Answers
Will Come

Answers Will Come

TRUSTING THE LORD
IN THE MEANTIME

SHALISSA
LINDSAY

Covenant Communications, Inc.

Cover image: *Compass on the Shore at Sunrise* © grapix, *Jigsaw Puzzle on Blue* © ThomasVogel, courtesy of istockphoto.com.

Cover design copyright © 2017 by Covenant Communications, Inc.

Published by Covenant Communications, Inc.
American Fork, Utah

Printed in the United States of America
First Printing: April 2017

23 22 21 20 19 18 17   10 9 8 7 6 5 4 3 2 1

ISBN 978-1-52440-190-0

This book is an expanded and revised version of the self-published title *On Things Not Seen: Perspectives for Trusting the Light*.

The text assumes reader familiarity with doctrines of The Church of Jesus Christ of Latter-day Saints. References made herein to scriptures and general conference addresses can be found in the Church's online archives available at www.lds.org.

Table of Contents

ACKNOWLEDGMENTS   IX

INTRODUCTION   XI

PART I

1. REMEMBERING A CRISIS OF QUESTIONING   I
   needed growth; biblical parallels; walking away from God; inventing my own God; fearful thing; behind the theoretical

2. BEGINNING TO GRASP THE ATONEMENT'S REACH   I5
   the main character; behind the words; what I forgot; still feeling it all; saints asked to endure; blessed wait; like dew

PART II

3. TREASURING FAITH OPPORTUNITIES   33
   tests for growing; math & fluency; the team can't; stronger than electricity; in the dark; more blessed; proof for miracles; already obtained; the gift of sacrifice; first promptings

4. RESOLVING INCONGRUITIES   55
   things I wouldn't do; pancake griddle; barbarian grandma; seeming contradictions; not-so-solid evidence

5. PONDERING PROPHETS' PERSPECTIVES   67
   occasional mistakes; seers living; forbidden to tell; babysitter's rules; missing miracles; WE, not THEY

6. VISUALIZING ETERNITY THROUGH METAPHORS   81
embryos and salsa; seed packets; 5,772 miles; saving to do BIG; already a CEO; musicians and octaves; scratches disappear

7. FINDING STRENGTH FOR OBEDIENCE   97
flight school; radon gas; blessings that never happened; visiting angel; for Jesus; the helping chair; showers for sheep; covenants that liberate

8. WINNING BRAIN BATTLES   117
mobile device streaming; hormones; rotting food; when in smoke; toddler vocabulary; translating for the Spirit; hurling mists of darkness; the accuser

9. CONCLUSION: WEIGHING GLORY   135
on the scale; knowing keeps growing; invisible glory; sparks; parting thought

SOURCES   147

Acknowledgments

Thanks forever to the family members who contributed countless hours of conversation and encouragement on this project from beginning to end. I cannot convey how deeply I have appreciated your insightful suggestions, your patience with multiple drafts, your wise and careful edits, and your loving enthusiasm. This includes many Andersons: EksAyn, Patty, EksAyn Aaron, Katie Marie, Leland, Trenton, Amber, Dallin, and Bryce together with Laura Checketts and Aubrey Brinkerhoff. Other family members I want to thank include Marian Lindsay, Kathleen Lindsay, Gordon Lindsay, Karl Stum, and Chandra Roberson.

I am especially indebted to EksAyn Aaron Anderson for orienting me on publishing; to Leland Anderson for the tutorial in stylistic editing; to Patty Anderson and Amber Anderson for additional intensive editing; to Emily Milner for mentoring me in tone to avoid unintended implications; and to Bryce Anderson for taking the book where it needed to go.

Many thanks to Kathryn Gordon, Samantha Millburn, Stephanie Lacy, and the staff at Covenant for their expertise and confidence in the message.

Special thanks to those family members or friends who taught me something herein but who did it so unselfishly and transparently that I received the gift and forgot the giver.

To Mom and Dad (Patty and EksAyn Anderson) and to my deceased mother, Linda Anderson: I honor your legacy of faithful questioning combined with covenant obedience. Thanks to my children for teaching me every day and for the joy of your perceptive questions and suggestions. I look forward to reading your books someday. Most of all, eternal thanks to my husband, Nathan, for seventeen years of unfailing support and for all the joy in our journey together. You were, and continue to be, the most magnificent answer to prayer that I have ever received.

Introduction

Even within The Church of Jesus Christ of Latter-day Saints, where continuing revelation illuminates so many questions, we don't have every piece to every puzzle.

When I was a young adult, my unanswered gospel questions threatened to overwhelm my testimony, choking my trust in God. I begged the Lord for doctrinal answers only He could give. Instead, He wisely offered me tutorials in trust. In this book, I share those in-the-meantime answers that for me have created intellectual breathing space. These ideas help me joyfully choose faith until all the answers come.

Today I am grateful beyond words for the blessings found in the Church. As online media increasingly bombards members with specific doubts and criticisms, I give thanks for wise doctrinal and historical responses from LDS scholars.[1] This book does not attempt to duplicate their work. Like me, they have usually concluded that reason and strong evidence support the Restoration of the gospel but that many specific questions still wait to be resolved through revelation.

Part I shares ideas that helped me navigate the first painful weeks of faith crisis, resolving to stay obedient and loyal to the Church. This section somewhat resembles a personal narrative but focuses specifically on the ideas themselves, which apply broadly beyond my own experience.

Part II shifts in tone to share individual perspectives that came later, a piece at a time over the next twenty years—not in dramatic plots but here and there, in quiet pondering and ordinary conversations. These bridge across chapter themes but do not continue as a connected narrative.

Because I know your time is precious, and often interrupted, I've confined each key idea to a single page.

May these perspectives strengthen you, or someone you love, as they have me.

PART I

CHAPTER I

Remembering a Crisis of Questioning

"[Christians], at their best, know that often they don't know. They do not have all the answers. They do not have God in their pocket. We cannot answer every question that any bright boy in the back row might ask. We have only light enough to walk by."

—Howard Johnson[2]

Needed growth can start
with a crisis of questions.

Darkness can set the stage
for light.

While considering serving a mission as a young adult, I enrolled in a BYU class called Mormon Issues. I thought it would prepare me to answer historical questions regarding The Church of Jesus Christ of Latter-day Saints.

Instead, it would prepare me in a different way, by requiring me to re-build my testimony from the ground up. Readings included the memoirs of an unhappy polygamous wife from the 1800s, together with more modern gender role debates. We also studied instances when Church leaders' state-ments had proven to be mistaken, as in the period before blacks received the priesthood in 1978. These readings burdened my heart.

I wrestled long and tearfully with these and related subjects, my faith sud-denly fragile and ill-equipped. I had been raised by parents who lived their testimonies with devotion. We had read the standard works multiple times and memorized many scripture passages. I had seen many answers to prayers. At home, church, and seminary, I had studied and appreciated the beautiful and holistic gospel landscape. Yet now I felt as though I had fallen on my face along the path and could see only gravel, which at close range looked more like boulders.

My questions didn't lurk casually in the background, at odd moments. Rather, they began pounding the moment I awoke and incessantly drummed in my brain throughout the day and past midnight. I heard and read answers that appeased others but didn't satisfy me. My tears often started even before my morning attempt at prayer and spilled over so unpredictably at all hours that I stopped wearing mascara. I felt at turns lonely, distrustful, foolish, numb, trapped by downward spiraling logic, and frustrated that God had not more fully resolved such important matters. How I carried on with classes and work, week after week, I can't remember.

Class debates merged with personal queries founded in private experiences. Mom had died and Dad was now sealed to both her and my stepmom. Several close college friends confided the ongoing fallout from their abusive childhoods. Identity-laden decisions about majors, mission, and marriage overwhelmed me. Some people I loved were in apostasy. I struggled to follow a local Church leader. This perilous season would force me to seek light like never before.

Most issues in Church history
have biblical parallels.

Some people who encounter hard questions in the Church decide simply to reject Joseph Smith, Brigham Young, and other latter-day leaders. They look for a new church to attend. But I could see no refuge elsewhere in Christianity. I accepted that the Catholic Church had strayed from Christ's original doctrine and that the break-off Protestant churches could not then have claim to any apostolic priesthood line of authority.

What's more, I realized that fleeing to another Christian church wouldn't resolve most of my doctrinal concerns since almost everything I had doubts about in Mormonism could also be seen in the Bible itself, once I looked carefully.

Modern prophets were not very different from biblical prophets; they were just uncomfortably close to us in years.

If I felt concern about polygamy, I could turn my back on Joseph Smith and other early prophets. But what about Abraham, Jacob, Moses, and Hannah, whom God approved? If I accepted the Bible, this doctrinal problem remained.

I didn't understand why prophets before 1978 had withheld the priesthood from some men based on race. But God Himself had segregated by lineage in the Bible. When 250 non-Levite princes demanded that Moses give them the priesthood, Jehovah burnt them with fire from heaven.[3] If I accepted the Bible, this doctrinal problem remained.

I could get upset that Apostles had several times preached mistaken personal opinions as doctrine. But I saw that God had frequently corrected biblical prophets without revoking their overall authority. God punished Moses for striking the rock for water instead of just speaking to it. Still, water came out as promised and Moses retained authority over the people.[4] God corrected Jonah's prejudice against the people in Nineveh quite sternly but still sent him to preach as a prophet.[5] The Apostles retained their authority even after Christ rebuked them for turning away the children,[6] arguing over who was greatest,[7] and calling for fire from heaven to consume the Samaritans.[8] This doctrinal problem remained.

And so it went for each concern.[9] Opting for another denomination, then, wouldn't satisfy me. I knew I needed to find resolution within the Church.

Walking away from God
creates its own hell.

Rejecting God altogether was really never an option. I had seen many answers to personal and family prayers by age twenty, and I was convinced of God's reality.

Still, I considered it briefly. The basic stance of many modern atheists is that if you're uncomfortable with the Bible, or with the notion of a God who allows or commands hard things, then just stop believing in both. Walk away from God altogether.

I saw in that direction an eventual wilderness where no one really matters and all is temporary and relative. The Bible is the bedrock of all Judeo-Christian beliefs about the sacredness of human life. The whole notion of fairness and personal rights derives from the conviction that there is a right and wrong. If the universe had no higher law (call it God), then my own "rights" would be irrelevant fancies of culture. They couldn't be sacred, because there would be no such thing as sacred. I would deserve nothing. Nobody would deserve anything because there would be no such thing as right and wrong.

For me, this alternative described a horrifying logical wasteland. Without absolute commandments, there is no compelling reason for humans not to exterminate people who oppose their own agenda. I'd heard atheists point to historical atrocities committed in the name of religion, but I saw atheist doctrines leading to far greater intolerance and violence. For example, over a period of 350 years, Catholicism's Spanish Inquisition executed an estimated 1,500–4,000 people for heresy. Yet atheist regimes executed 100,000,000 people in just the twentieth century.[10] In the absence of God's laws, killing, stealing, and adultery all become optional conveniences.

At a personal level, if I rejected God, I could pray to no one. There would be no reason to marry or have children beyond momentary expediency. And if I did anyway, I would have no reason to expect reunion after death. There would be no hope that this life's wrongs would be resolved in justice hereafter.

If I rejected God and dismissed heaven as irrelevant, I would still be inherently choosing the hell that remained. I was not going to find satisfying peace or purpose without God still in the picture.

Inventing
my own God
would cause me to lose
the real One.

I waded through essays by religious authors trying to explain away doctrinal areas they didn't like. Some deconstructed tough Biblical passages as purely figurative, exaggerations, or instructive propaganda distorted by historians. They often viewed latter-day events and scripture with similar lenses.

To me, this kind of doctrinal quicksand just detoured through agnosticism on its way back toward atheism. I allowed for a few omissions and errors, such as the handful of Bible passages corrected by the Joseph Smith Translation. But without divine revelation, I could see no coherent, consistent way to explain away all the hard parts without also undermining all the beautiful parts along the way.

Uncomfortable things were inconveniently tied to beautiful corollaries. For example, dismissing harsh commandments in the law of Moses also undermines the divinity behind laws to protect women and children from abuse and the poor from exploitation. Abandoning the fierce God who destroys the wicked also abandons the just, merciful God who rescues victims from brutal child sacrifice and slave trafficking.

I became frustrated with writers who downplayed miracles reportedly witnessed by multitudes. *Maybe* a single earthquake or plague could be coincidental—but repeated fire from heaven? Or 185,000 Assyrians falling dead overnight?[11] I was convinced that ancient Jews had sufficient contemporary witnesses and evidence to consider these events as more than fantastic self-spun fairy tales. Likewise, hundreds of testimonies asserted the Kirtland Temple Pentecost, the prophetic mantle falling on Brigham Young,[12] and so on.

I wanted God to "soften around the edges" for my own comfort, but I didn't want to fashion an imaginary God after my own preferred image. In a choose-your-own-God buffet, I might gravitate toward dessert but, in doing so, forfeit essential nutrition from other less tasty staples. If I tried to redefine the God I would accept—one who wouldn't upset my sensibilities—I might unwittingly lose the best parts of Him altogether.

I thought often of C.S. Lewis's assertion about the fictional Christ-figure, Aslan: "He's not a *tame* lion."

"It is a fearful thing
to fall into the hands
of the living God."
—Hebrews 10:31

Over several weeks, I prayed and cried through boxes of Kleenex, swarmed by depressing thoughts about the historical and doctrinal areas in question.

One day between classes, walking past the library and looking at the clouds, I realized that I couldn't sidestep my confrontation with God any longer. I had started out wondering whether prophets could be trusted—even harboring some hard feelings toward Joseph and Brigham over a few incidents. But in that moment, I realized that shooting the messengers wouldn't solve any of my concerns. It was just a distraction that allowed me to avoid the prickly position of pointing fingers at the Ruler of the Universe.

But there it was. I was upset at God.

No amount of prophetic weakness[13] could remove the fact that *God* had delayed full resolution on key issues, both then and now. Despite His demonstrated ability to resolve things through crystal-clear revelation, and despite His obvious ability to correct a prophet, He had chosen to let His servants and devoted Saints struggle messily with hard problems and unanswered questions. How could I trust Him when He sometimes allowed—or even commanded—His Saints to undergo confusion, hardship, injustice, and sorrow?

I could abandon modern-day prophets altogether. I could declare that I would only accept personal revelation. But if I genuinely allowed that God might speak at all—even if only to me instead of to a prophet—I must reconcile with the distinct possibility that He could respond in ways I didn't like, on a time frame I didn't like, and require things I didn't like.

Even faithful Abraham, Moses, Isaiah, Jeremiah, Peter, and Paul were all asked by God to accept hard things they didn't want to do.

What's more, God could let hard things unfold in my life whether or not I believed in Him. Whether or not I followed Him. Whether or not I acknowledged His prophets. Even if I were angry at Him or turned my back on Him. God would forever, by definition, have the power to put hard things in my life, or remove them at will. I needed to face Him.

Behind many
theoretical questions
hides a personal one.

Most of the specific situations I had considered were tentacles of the age-old human question, "How can God allow suffering?"[14] Now, I realized that underneath all the doctrinal and historical questions hid my real concern:

What will God require me *to suffer? Will He treat* me *like Job? Require Abrahamic-like sacrifices? Intervene to protect* me*? Or not? What will God demand of* me*?*

Deep down, I was scared of the God of difficult things. What sacrifices would be demanded by my upcoming mission call? Mosquito nets? A third-world disease? And afterward, what if I never married? Or my husband died early? Or I died early and he remarried? Or my children had handicaps? Or so many other difficult possibilities. . . .

I wanted to make temple covenants of obedience and consecration, but I had no control over what God might ask in my future, and He offered no guarantees. It seemed so unfair. How could I surrender my future to Him, even my eternal life, when I couldn't control where that might lead?

I marveled that some blacks had been baptized and stayed loyal to the Church in the years before they could receive the priesthood or temple ordinances, undeterred by misapplied doctrine and racism still among white members. How did they handle the spiritual despair, the unanswered doctrinal implications for eternity? Didn't they feel God was unfair for not setting it right sooner? How did they still trust Him?

For a research paper, I examined the question. Interviews with black members[15] revealed that in the face of all those issues, they had held tightly to comforting spiritual assurances from God Himself that they were known and valued individually. Some recounted amazing priesthood blessings. Some had heard the Lord's voice direct them in specific words. Some had been bathed in majestic love and comfort during their prayers. They relied on these sweet experiences, humbly following prophets and waiting patiently through trials until the promised further light arrived.

I wanted to learn the powerful trust that sustained those early black members. I wanted to feel that same security in God's love for me individually. I just didn't know how to start.

CHAPTER 2

Beginning to Grasp the Atonement's Reach

"Thus, the Savior has suffered not just for our sins and iniquities—but also for our physical pains and anguish, our weaknesses and shortcomings, our fears and frustrations, our disappointments and discouragement, our regrets and remorse, our despair and desperation, the injustices and inequities we experience, and the emotional distresses that beset us.

"There is no physical pain, no spiritual wound, no anguish of soul or heartache, no infirmity or weakness you or I ever confront in mortality that the Savior did not experience first."

—Elder David A. Bednar[16]

Every Book of Mormon story
has the same main character.

One day, I admitted to my visiting teachers that I didn't relate to people who referred to Jesus as their close, personal friend. It made sense to me that Heavenly Father could be a best friend because He listened to and answered prayers. But Christ's suffering for my sins was two thousand years ago. I was grateful for that. But I never talked to Him, and He didn't talk to me. How could that be an active friendship?

My visiting teachers encouraged me to get a yellow highlighter and start rereading the Book of Mormon with a single goal in mind: to find every detail about Jesus—every symbol of Him, everything He spoke, and everything that described Him or His actions.

Then these two sisters[17] gently taught me something I had never fully appreciated before. Whenever the Book of Mormon mentions the Lord, it refers to Jehovah, just as in the Old Testament. And Jehovah is Jesus Christ.

So in 1 Nephi 1:1 when it says, "Having been highly favored of the Lord in all my days," I should read it as "Having been highly favored of the *Lord Jesus Christ* in all my days."

And when Nephi says, "The Lord had delivered Laban into my hands,"[18] I should mentally read it as "The *Lord Jesus Christ* had delivered Laban into my hands."

I realized I had largely treated the term *Lord* like a vague positive sentiment. I'd read it as though it said "providence delivered Laban" or "good fortune delivered Laban." I hadn't seen Jesus Christ Himself involved intimately in these verses.

The next day, I bought a new paperback copy of the Book of Mormon and started highlighting. I read intently. Not one or two chapters a day but ten or fifteen or twenty. I could not believe how many pages were totally yellow, even hundreds of pages before I reached the book of 3 Nephi. For the first time, I saw Jesus Christ, page after page, chapter after chapter. He participated in the wilderness journeys. He actively arranged affairs within the war chapters. I saw Jesus Christ protecting the innocent and offering to heal the wicked. He was the main character in every story, caring deeply about the details in people's lives.

His power is behind the words.
Silent. Real.

Highlighting anew the Book of Mormon brought to my attention many direct quotes from the Lord Jesus Christ Himself. I began to notice that every so often, I felt subtle power behind those specific passages. I don't know how to describe it except to say that here and there, as I searched for Him specifically, I began to feel Jesus Christ directly convey a few verses to me on a spiritual level.

I can only compare it to something that sometimes happens in movies. The heroine will be reading a letter from someone, perhaps her beau. She begins reading in her own voice, but within the first few lines, the audio producer blends in the man's voice and the action continues with him describing details in his own voice.

It was like that, except there were no sounds. It wasn't even really the verbal voice in my head. It was a spiritual feeling separate from me. It was not a warmth in the chest as I've heard other people describe. For me, there was no physical sensation whatsoever. Most of the time, I read in my own voice. But sometimes, for some passages, I could feel the words being sort of read to me in spirit by a spiritual voice different from my own. I perceived that Jesus Christ was very alive and present and connected to me. And that He was fully aware that I was reading in that moment.

On prior occasions I had sometimes felt a scripture "speak to me," but I hadn't really identified the feeling as a speaker. Perhaps I thought of it as my own conscience vaguely amplified by the Holy Ghost. Now I began to identify that feeling as coming, in real time, from Jesus Christ to me. I had felt the call/voice/message of the Lord Jesus Christ before but without realizing it. The living Jesus Christ had actually spoken to me, at times even before I knew who was speaking. Now I began, however haltingly, to recognize that feeling as His voice. It was for me as the Lord described:

"Behold, that which you hear is as the voice of one crying in the wilderness—in the wilderness, because you cannot see him—my voice, because my voice is Spirit; my Spirit is truth."[19]

Protesting to God
about the injustice of suffering,
I had forgotten.
It was His pain too.

One morning, the newspaper contained an account of wo
been gang raped and tortured during the Serbian civil war. I c
ably for two hours because I knew it wasn't just happening on other conti-
nents. That same month, two girlfriends had independently confided in me
about the abuse they had suffered as children. It was too much. Again I asked
how I could possibly trust in God's love and goodness when He permitted so
much evil, injustice, and suffering?

Here the Book of Mormon boldly declares an answer beyond those
found in the world. Christ did not merely suffer the penalties for our sins.
He also took upon Himself "the pains of every living creature, both men,
women, and children, who belong to the family of Adam."[20] This includes
sicknesses, afflictions, temptations, infirmities, griefs, sorrows, and "the
chastisement of our peace."[21]

We rightfully hate it that God has sent innocent babies to abusive
homes. It should awe us that Jesus essentially sent Himself into every one
of those homes too. He has endured every rape and every torture Himself.
Heavenly Father didn't just send His Son to die for us collectively. He sent
His Son to feel the daily pains and the death pangs of every separate child,
woman, or man who ever lived. In the Garden of Gethsemane, Jesus tran-
scended time and space to somehow accompany every individual soul on
his or her private journey through evil and pain. He felt it all with each one
of us.

He has looked out through the tearful eyes of those struggling to understand or live with same-sex attraction. He knows the hopeless heartache when that last-resort in vitro fails—again. He has felt bipolar mood
swings. He has undergone all our chemotherapies, the sting of divorce
proceedings, our rejections and devastating failures. Jesus knows the empty
parking lot or dark closet where we cry. He knows the aching knees and
puffy eyes after we run out of tears but not questions. These are His pains
too.

He knows what He's asking of us. Of me. He knows it fully. Personally.
Intimately.

Jesus hasn't forgotten
how much it hurts.
In a sense,
He is still feeling it all.

At some point, it dawned on me that I could speak of the Atonement in present rather than past tense. True, that victory is 100 percent complete, finalized, an absolute historical fact. Christ said, "It is finished." Yet Christ also says "time only is measured unto men" and "all things are present with me, for I know them all."[22] Because Jesus remembers all things as present, He can still be in the very thick of our experiences, swallowing the pain with us, here and now, whatever we are suffering. He says, "Behold, I have graven thee upon the palms of my hands; thy walls are continually before me."[23]

In this verse, the words *thee* and *thy* are singular terms (not the plural terms, *ye* and *your*). Here, the Lord is not talking collectively to a group of people. He is talking to every one of us as an individual, one at a time.

Just as easily as I call to mind a remembered melody, Jesus can and does have wholly present in His mind and heart the full import of whatever troubles I'm living through. His knowledge is not just intellectual or sympathetic but rather graven on the cells and sinews and spiritual depths of His own soul in a permanent, ownership kind of way.

He doesn't just watch our pain. It is continually before Him. He aches with it. He weeps with us. He bleeds with us. He reels with the fears and the confusion. He throbs with the hurt we feel. Even when we are angry at Him.

He sees, from our viewpoint, the intellectual walls that block our understanding. He sees the physical limitations that keep us from activities we desire. He sees the social and cultural walls we put up between people. He sees them from our side of the wall. He feels our pains and limited understanding. We literally cannot suffer anything alone, no matter how victimized we may try to feel in our weak moments.

When Christ asks His Saints
to endure hard or painful things,
He suffers the full impact Himself.

Understanding the Atonement helped me cope with tough spots in Church history and the Old Testament. I still didn't completely understand Jehovah's overall purposes, but I did manage to see that His voluntary acceptance of our everyday suffering undeniably showed His love.

Whenever Christ has given a commandment that demanded suffering or sacrifice (from self-denial to imprisonment to martyrdom), He has taken that painful trouble upon Himself as well. He felt the damp prison with Jeremiah. He knows the searing flame experienced by Abinadi. He suffered the destruction along with every Jew sent captive to Babylon and the punishment with every soul who died in Jericho.

Christ required the pioneers to cross the plains. Therefore, His Atonement had to include that suffering too: Christ has felt the pain of bloody footsteps, the grief of burying babies along the way, and the sting of icy river crossings.

Through the Atonement, Christ has personally experienced plural marriage from the vantage point of the fifth wife, and the first wife, and every individual concubine of ancient times. He Himself has passed through every painful struggle related to this commandment.

In Gethsemane, Jesus walked in the shoes of each black child of God withheld from priesthood and temple blessings. He knows the humiliation of segregation and discrimination from the inside out, not only in these cases but in slave galleys and gas chambers and every other case throughout human history.

He fully comprehends how lonely it can be to live the law of chastity when others are getting married or giving in to temptations. He has felt the hopeless bewilderment, loneliness, and heartache when eternal companions don't appear or when same-sex attraction prevents someone from moving toward marriage.

I cannot begin to comprehend Jesus Christ's reasons for asking us to pass through these types of trials. But even though I don't understand, I can no longer claim that Christ is unfair for requiring them. He suffered them all too.

A blessed wait
is also an answer.

When I left on my mission, many of my deepest questions for God persisted. But I now had a clear testimony of the Book of Mormon and a fresh appreciation for Jesus Christ's Atonement. I was anxious to share it.

Interestingly, I was called to the Brazil São Paulo South Mission. Because interracial marriage abounds there, most citizens had black heritage, which had been an obstacle to the spread of the Church before 1978. In hindsight, I could see that my pre-mission questions had prepared me very specifically for conversations and situations I would encounter in São Paulo.

My time in Brazil provided thought-provoking examples of racism, gender roles, language barriers, socioeconomic inequities, addictions, and abuse. God had sent me to a place where I could better ponder the nuances related to so many of the questions I'd had already. Some of my questions were answered, and in turn new ones replaced them.

What I was unprepared for was the joy. It would come upon me at almost random moments, such as when we walked up a hill overlooking the little tin roof homes in my area. On one ordinary day, perhaps even a little drizzly, there suddenly blossomed within me an incredible affirmation that I was literally an ambassador authorized by Jesus Christ—that I carried the most important truths in the whole world. Nothing more happened. I was just bursting with joy, praise, conviction, confidence, and deep gratitude to be allowed to work with these people, at this time, in this place. I wanted to sing and shout and hug everyone and stay forever.

In my final area, just a month before returning home, I stood one morning in the bathroom, getting ready for the day. One of my old questions kept swirling through my brain, and I mentally asked it again. In that ordinary moment, a few words entered my mind with absolute clarity. It was an angle I had never considered, and I was suddenly at peace with that particular query.

To me, as important as the answer itself was the manner in which it arrived, personalized to me. God had heard me! I felt keenly that He would answer additional questions if I would diligently try to cultivate more unyielding faith in Him.

Like dew,
living water
arrives quietly.

Answers Will Come

Twenty years have passed now, full of more spiritual joys than anticipated. Being a wife and mother has been more rewarding than I ever guessed it could be. Church membership has blessed me with growth, friendships, and joyful service opportunities. I've solved some of my old questions and encountered many new ones. Periodically, new crises, misgivings, and concerns arise, so my list of queries for the Lord is as long as ever. But now I frame them within the context of many personal experiences with His goodness.

Sometimes a flash of insight downloads through the Spirit. A few of my questions have been answered through personal sacred experiences, rare and precious. Most of the final answers are still pending and may not arrive until Christ returns.

Meanwhile, I have discovered the truth that "the doctrine of the priesthood shall distil upon thy soul as the dews from heaven."[24] Over time, in that gradual, incremental process, I've been granted clarity and certainty that Christ called Joseph Smith, sent the Book of Mormon, and continues to guide the Church today in impressively intimate detail. The Lord has offered me a multitude of quiet reassurances that I can trust Him. That I can find joy in His Church. That He has planned magnificent resolutions for my concerns. These in-the-meantime answers have come packaged with great variety, but each conveys the message, *"Here's another reason to trust Me."*

In the coming pages, I share some of these reassurances. They include metaphors, analogies, and lines of reasoning that help me feel peace amid many suspended questions until further light comes. For me, they allow intellectual breathing space in areas where I can't yet see the answers.

Where possible, I try to share the context from my life in which I grasped a certain principle. But many ideas arrived as silently as dew condenses on morning grass. I can't remember how I learned them or who taught them to me. Had I intended to write a book (I never considered it), I might have more faithfully recorded the detailed circumstances surrounding some of the other "aha!" moments. I ask for forgiveness, therefore, that I cannot connect all the dots into a single story line.

PART II

CHAPTER 3

Treasuring Faith Opportunities

"With even your strongest faith, God will not always reward you immediately according to your desires. Rather, God will respond with what in His eternal plan is best for you, when it will yield the greatest advantage. Be thankful that sometimes God lets you struggle for a long time before that answer comes. That causes your faith to increase and your character to grow."

—Elder Richard G. Scott[25]

The test isn't
what I know.
It's how I grow.

We sometimes dissect the purposes of life into a few separate sentences. To obtain bodies. To be tested. To become more like God. I think they are inseparably connected: our bodies are part of the testing, and the process of testing is inherently designed to perfect us.

I am convinced that God's tests differ significantly from college entrance exams. They are not crafted to separate out the brightest students for entrance into heaven.

I believe His tests are of the developmental sort, specifically designed to cultivate growth in every child willing to undergo them. Human beings willingly submit to developmental testing in many contexts:

(1) Musical performances before an adjudicator

Often sponsored by a music teachers' association, this evaluation partly tests the student's preparation, but is mostly designed to increase students' confidence in their own ability to perform.

(2) Product stress testing

Engineers submit inventions for iterative stress testing. When weakness is found, the product is then adjusted and reinforced for increased strength or resilience in the future.

(3) Qualifying exams for a PhD (in some social sciences)

For this long research paper (of fifty to a hundred pages), students collect and summarize all the research related to the question they plan to study for their dissertation. The students acquire the subject matter expertise as they work through the exam. When the faculty committee considers the collected research sufficiently extensive, the student "passes" the exam. The paper then becomes part of the first chapters of the student's dissertation.

In each example above, the test itself provides growth and specific preparation for the next stage of work. So perhaps my tests are as much about preparing for an eternal future as they are about evaluating my preparation from the past.

Spiritual fluency
comes from frequent,
repeated tests.

At this particular stage in my life, I've begun to think that God is testing me the same way elementary schools teach multiplication tables. After learning the basic answers, kids begin timed quizzes to help them increase in fluency. How many times tables can they get right in five minutes? And the next week? And the next week? Getting faster yet?

The teacher is less concerned with today's absolute scores than with the measurable progress of each student. These tests aren't designed for the teacher's benefit in evaluation. They are designed for the growth of the student.

I seem to be working on spiritual fluency by drilling through lots of repetitious testing on the same basic questions:

Will I control the flesh? *When hungry? tired? pregnant? sick? imbalanced? in a rush? flooded by adrenaline?*

Will I choose to love? *siblings? neighbors? children? spouse? Regardless of difficulty? inconvenience? offenses? language barriers? age? social group? race? economic status?*

Will I love God first? *More than myself? friends? family? money? leisure? convenience? honors? pet projects?*

Will I believe and trust Him? *Even if it's painful? unfair? boring? slow? confusing? unpopular?*

For each category, I've given some correct responses, but I'm not fluent yet. As I keep testing, I hope to get better.

As I exercise control over my body, I become more disciplined. As I push past barriers to love, I become more loving. As I sacrifice for God, I grow closer to Him. As I practice trusting Him, I grow powerful in my ability to summon faith.

The conditions that test my willingness to love can also stretch and expand my ability to love. The conditions that test my faith can also grow my faith. This may be a large part of why I was willing to submit to testing. I really wanted to come out better—more like my Heavenly Parents.

This chapter focuses particularly on what I've learned about faith. It explores why faith is so valuable that it's worth enduring all this testing.

Faith in yourself
and in the team
can't make resurrected bodies.

Even people with no religion exercise faith in worldly things. We all do. We brush our teeth to avoid cavities. We save for retirement. We put on snow tires to stay ahead of the coming weather. We plant seeds and water them until harvest. We diet, exercise, and plan vacations. We work and study hard, trusting in the payoffs.

This kind of faith is powerful, real, and necessary. It involves action and trust in people or natural processes. It builds bridges, creates banks, leads to inventions, composes music, and persuades people to join a cause. It obtains all kinds of sought-after results: gold medals, fame, wealth.

All of God's children benefit from repeatedly exercising this kind of faith, and our capacities grow intellectually, socially, emotionally, academically, and professionally. We learn that actions, belief, and patience can yield great results.

But worldly faith can only obtain things *in this world.* No amount of raw action and belief can secure the eternal things we deeply and desperately want:

A world without decay, fear, and loss

Resurrected, perfect bodies

Families happily united forever

Endless knowledge and power

Only Jesus Christ has the power to secure these eternal things for us. We will never get them unless He gives them to us. We cannot just have faith in ourselves, our hard work, or the ingenuity of science. We must have faith in Him, on His terms, as defined by His covenants.

We exercise faith in Christ when our determination to believe and obey Him begins, however falteringly, to supersede other mortal enticements. We then begin to be unmoved by external circumstances to the point that, eventually, we are never again externally controlled. Sometimes in trickles, sometimes in gushes, Christ's power cascades into our lives to wash us, refresh us, buoy us up, and carry us. Over time, it infuses into our souls tremendous amounts of wisdom, pure love, and lasting joy.

Hereafter, when I write faith, I mean *faith in Christ.*

We left heaven, in part,
to master a power
stronger than electricity.

This fallen world is perfectly designed to bewilder us with pain, failed logic, confusion, conflict, injustice, and doubt. If intellectual certainty about spiritual things were the goal, we definitely would have stayed in heaven.

Instead, we shouted for joy at the upcoming chance to live with our spiritual eyes blindfolded.[26] Coming to earth—and embracing the limitations of the veil—is exactly the opposite of requiring answers and immediate solutions. For some reason, we really looked forward to having our faith tested. I think that's because we understood that, if we were humble, testing our faith would make it stronger.

But why would even strong faith be worth so much distress? Joseph Smith's *Lectures on Faith* describes faith as the power "by which the worlds were framed . . . by which Jehovah works, and through which he exercises power over all temporal as well as eternal things."[27]

Elder Boyd K. Packer said: "The kind of faith that is worthy and prepared and unyielding . . . *calls forth things that otherwise would not be.* It is the kind of faith that moves people. It is the kind of faith that sometimes moves things. . . . *It is a marvelous, even a transcendent, power, a power as real and as invisible as electricity.* Directed and channeled, it has great effect."[28]

And Elder Neil L. Andersen added: "Faith in the Lord Jesus Christ is not something ethereal, floating loosely in the air. . . . It is, as the scriptures say, "substance, the evidence of things not seen" (Hebrews 11:1). *Faith emits a spiritual light, and that light is discernible* (see Alma 32:35)"[29]

Faith goes beyond praying through our daily challenges and waiting for heaven. Faith is pure, eternal, godly power. Planet-creating power. Orbit-governing power. Blind-healing, mountain-moving, sea-dividing, raising-the-dead, fire-from-heaven kind of power. Learning to summon the power of faith during trials was so important that we were willing to brave every earthly darkness, including and especially the opportunities to doubt that would surround us at every corner.

We practice best
in the dark.

We really didn't come to earth to witness God's miraculous power. We were already familiar with that. Instead, we came to earth partly to practice walking by faith, in the dark. As we develop our faith—along with humility, patience, and charity—we grow toward the celestial people our Father intends us to be: one day capable of performing magnificent miracles ourselves in the eternities, powerful beyond imagination.

If faith comes too easily or automatically, it will not be strong enough. By definition, faith requires not seeing, not understanding, often feeling confused or even trapped. So earth life has to be hard. Really hard. Every time we push past doubt and difficulty, our faith in Christ multiplies. For now, miracles have to be the rare exception. Answers have to come slowly. God constantly withholds miracles He could easily perform and answers He could easily give.

He could have given manna to Nephi's family in the wilderness. He could have fed the Jaredite families with just five loaves and two fishes. But think how much faith both groups had to exercise while repeatedly gathering provisions.

We occasionally keep children from using their money for short-term reasons because we know it will be better spent when it has built up to a meaningful level. I've wondered: does the Lord sometimes make me wait for certain miracles so that the "principal balance" of my faith can grow exponentially, as though with interest?

Peter said, "The trial of your faith, [is] much more precious than of gold."[30] As God delays answers and miracles, He offers us the time to weave increasingly powerful faith into the permanent patterns and habits of our souls.

When our faith in Christ amasses to the critical level, our mortal restrictions can someday be removed. Like Nephi and the brother of Jared, we can one day have sufficient faith to handle the responsibilities associated with meeting the Savior and experiencing the visions that explain everything.

"Faith is things which are hoped for and not seen; wherefore, dispute not because ye see not, for ye receive no witness until after the trial of your faith."[31]

Not having all the answers
is more blessed.

In our quest for faith, The Church of Jesus Christ of Latter-day Saints is a tremendous and indispensable asset. But not because it offers all the answers to every possible question. Even—perhaps especially—within the restored gospel, there have to be some opportunities for us to question and doubt. They provide the opposition against which faith can grow and strengthen. In fact, Christ has deliberately withheld some things for this express purpose.[32] He told Mormon, "I will try the faith of my people."[33]

Hence, the Lord supports faith but does not demand it. He lets us discover substantial internal evidences in latter-day scriptures but withholds incontrovertible proof. He gives us eleven witnesses of the gold plates but leaves Book of Mormon geography uncertain. By not compelling us to believe, Christ offers us the chance to be "more blessed." He told the Nephites who had seen him that "more blessed are they who shall believe in your words because that ye shall testify that ye have seen me."[34]

And He told his doubting Apostle Thomas, "Blessed are they that have not seen, and yet have believed."[35]

Apparently, the growth we gain from believing without seeing is so valuable that it's worth delaying a visit from the Savior. We, too, considered it "more blessed" to practice believing in the dark. That's why we left the sure knowledge we already had in our premortal existence.

Perhaps this is why the Lord doesn't simply foil more attacks against the Church by revealing the answers. We know He did stop one attempt to discredit the Book of Mormon. When the first 116 translated pages were lost to Joseph Smith, the Lord pointed out that He'd had Nephi make a second version of the record 2,400 years earlier.[36] He explained, "Satan thinketh to overpower your testimony . . . that the work may not come forth . . . [but] I will not suffer that they shall destroy my work; . . . my wisdom is greater than the cunning of the devil."[37]

Apparently, Christ doesn't consider today's remaining anti-Mormon ploys sufficiently powerful to stop His work. They must provide the perfect mix of confusion to develop our faith.

Heavenly silence is not
a proof against miracles
but a proof in favor of them.

Korihor claimed that spiritual experiences were "the effect of a frenzied mind."[38] When answers or miracles finally come, how will I know they're from God, rather than from my own self-deception, hypnosis, or positive thinking?

I'll know, partly, because I've tried really hard to produce them, with no success. Trust me, if I could hypnotize myself into receiving heavenly answers, I'm pretty sure I would have done it dozens of times by now. It doesn't work. Much to my chagrin, my prayers, fasting, and temple trips are often met with silence. I've learned I really have little control over when and how heaven answers my prayers. I simply can't conjure up that amazing peace whenever I want it. Self-talk during my prayers just doesn't feel like those answers that have come on special occasions. No matter how hard I try.

Because we have repeatedly met silence, when the eventual answer comes, it feels clearly different. We recognize those special messages from the Lord precisely because they are rare and unusual and come at unexpected intervals. They feel so very different from the anguished or circular thought patterns that we create ourselves.

The woman who touched Jesus's robe recognized her miraculous healing because she had tried everything she could for twelve years— without success! The pregnancies of aged Sarah and Elizabeth were exceptionally miraculous because they took exceptionally long to occur. Alma and Amulek "could not be confined in dungeons," but "they did not exercise their power until they were bound in bands and cast into prison . . . that the Lord might show forth his power."[39]

I've heard it said, *"The prerequisite for a miracle is great difficulty; the prerequisite for a great miracle is impossibility."*[40] The difficulties and impossibilities are shown during the silence that precedes the miracle. Miraculous answers, when they come, will be clear and recognizable precisely because of the wait today. We are already in the process. It has already begun. The silence today is part of the miracle tomorrow.

I've already obtained
the answer.
I just haven't seen it yet.

I trust that my online orders at Amazon.com will be fulfilled because I receive an e-mail telling me so, and I believe it. The Lord's version of a "shipping confirmation" is even better:

> Verily I say unto you my friends, fear not, let your hearts be comforted; yea, rejoice evermore, and in everything give thanks;
>
> Waiting patiently on the Lord, for *your prayers have entered into the ears of the Lord of Sabaoth, and are recorded with this seal and testament—the Lord hath sworn and decreed that they shall be granted.*
>
> Therefore, he giveth this promise unto you, with an immutable covenant that they shall be fulfilled; and all things wherewith you have been afflicted shall work together for your good, and to my name's glory, saith the Lord.[41]

Heaven's fulfillments must be at least as trustworthy as Amazon's. The Lord told Nephi—2,416 years ahead of time—the exact words He would speak during Joseph Smith's First Vision.[42] The whole vision was planned in every detail, ready to deliver as soon as Joseph was ready. Likewise, Lehi considered God's fulfillment so certain that even before his wilderness journey, while still in a tent, he declared, "I have obtained a land of promise, in the which things I do rejoice."[43]

God likely has many answers already beautifully packaged and on the way to me. I bet He doesn't mind if I keep eagerly checking the mail, but I shouldn't be accusing Him of neglecting to send the answer. *Ensign* writer Adam Kotter[44] pointed out that this is essentially the difference between gospel questioning (good) and faithless doubting (bad):

Questioner: "There must be an answer to this question. I'll keep obeying until I see it."

Doubter: "I doubt there's an answer to this. I'm not obeying unless/until I can see it."

With that in mind, I want to say with other believers, "I have questions but no doubts."[45] I also want to learn to pray, *in advance*, the same way I respond when someone tells me they have sent a gift in the mail: "Thank you so much! I'm sure it will be great."

When faith is too weak
for a blessing,
God increases it
through sacrifice.

Let's say God wants to send me a huge, miraculous blessing, but my faith isn't strong enough to receive it. What will prepare me for the upcoming gift? President Harold B. Lee declared, "I [am] persuaded of one great truth: Whenever the Lord has a great blessing for one of his children, he puts that son or daughter in the way to make a great sacrifice."[46]

I have seen this happen with small sacrifices, too. I was once prompted to befriend a woman who seemed very needy. Feeling overwhelmed with the demands in my own family, I hesitated. But I obeyed. This sister later blessed us with many hours of babysitting. The "sacrifice" God prompted me to make ultimately blessed me as much as it did her.

A family I know prayed hard to be able to handle the upcoming student loans for graduate school. They felt, unexpectedly, that they should contribute generously to the Church's Perpetual Education Fund to help some far less fortunate student. After following that prompting, they received such a large funding offer that student loans became unnecessary. They felt certain that God's gift was linked to their willingness to sacrifice.

The widow of Zarephath needed to feed Elija before she could receive miraculous food for the famine and the healing of her dead son.[47] Adam needed to sacrifice animals to receive additional direction.[48] Peter, James, John, and Andrew had to leave their nets to become Apostles.[49] Early Saints needed to build a temple so they could receive their endowments.[50]

Chances to build faith come more often as tiny inconvenient sacrifices than grand gestures that earn public praise. How many minutes will I divert from other pursuits to spend time in family history research and indexing? How many leisure hours will I devote to callings and missionary work?

Lehi sacrificed part of his recently gathered provisions in a voluntary offering of gratitude.[51] Ancient Saints worshipped by presenting voluntary thank offerings at the temple.[52] When I'm grateful enough to *volunteer* extra resources or temple service, I may more fully approach the level of faith that allows for greater opportunities ahead.

If I heed the first prompting,
I might be given more.

One day in the car, I sat fuming about an incident with a woman whom I felt had manipulated me. As I finished my errand, I started absentmindedly humming a little melodic phrase, about sixteen notes long, over and over. I couldn't think of the words but eventually identified the melody as part of some sacrament hymn, though I couldn't remember which one. Realizing that it must be a prompting, I spent some time searching through the hymnbook for the notes tugging on my brain. I finally located them, tucked away in the third verse of "Reverently and Meekly Now."[53] These words were the Savior's gentle invitation for me to repent: *"Oh, forgive as thou wouldst be e'en forgiven now by me."* When I followed the Lord's counsel, that woman became a treasured friend.

This is just one of several times that heavenly direction has come to me through a half-remembered strain of music. I'm learning that revelation often requires me to pay full attention to the first clue if I want to find more. This happens with scripture too.

On another occasion, a family situation required me to choose between two radically different alternatives. I felt my decision depended entirely upon whether our family circumstances were permanent or temporary, and I prayed for inspiration. A single phrase came to mind. *"I know the thoughts that I think toward you."*[54] When I searched for these words in the Gospel Library database, I found Jeremiah instructing the exiled Jews to act as though their exile to Babylon was permanent, because it would last for seventy years. Several details in that long chapter spoke to me specifically. But the Lord did not download the whole chapter for me. He offered a single line and waited for me to seek more.

This pattern of piece-by-piece revelation appears everywhere in scripture. Joseph Smith had to act on James 1:5 before he received the First Vision. The Lord prompted Nephi to "Arise, and get thee into the mountain"[55] before he gave ship-building instructions. Like them, I may find that I have to follow the first promptings to ponder a verse, or visit the "mountain of the Lord" before I receive the instructions I need most.

CHAPTER 4

Resolving Incongruities

"In that day when the Lord shall come, he shall reveal all things . . .
hidden things which no man knew."

—D&C 101:32–33

It's a good thing
God does things
I wouldn't.

Would I really want a God whose purposes were so clear to me that I could perfectly understand them and explain them to others?

No way!

What a disaster *that* would be. That would make Him no smarter than I am. I wouldn't worship that God and neither would you.

I only want to worship God if He understands everything I don't. It's good if He does things I wouldn't think of doing. Or does them differently than I would. If I am on track in worshiping the real, all-knowing, all-powerful God, then I will necessarily (and happily) find times when His purposes are utterly incomprehensible to me. He may do things I don't like at all for reasons I don't yet accept or can't begin to imagine.

Meanwhile, it would be silly for me to stop following His instructions just because I don't precisely understand them.

Imagine the catastrophe if I used that logic with the rest of my life. I'd have to avoid indoor plumbing until I mastered the city's chemical treatment plan. I'd have to skip using appliances until I examined every circuit. I'd have to delay medical treatment until I'd read every scientific journal. I'd have to delete all software if I couldn't inspect the code.

In reality, I trust many things that I don't perfectly understand. I frequently put my life in the hands of total strangers. Airline pilots. Food manufacturers. Electricians. Every driver on the road. These people know a lot that I don't know. I trust them sufficiently that I usually don't demand detailed explanations for all their actions.

Peace doesn't depend on understanding God's reasons for doing what He does. Hopefully, they're so far above me that it would be pointless for Him to try to explain them to me. For me, peace comes from remembering reasons why I can trust His wisdom and goodness. Things like planetary orbits, balanced ecosystems, and newborn babies. Wonderful things I barely understand.

"For as the heavens are higher than the earth, so are my ways higher than your ways, and my thoughts than your thoughts."[56]

A pancake griddle,
unplugged,
can still burn you.

I'm learning it's okay if I can't satisfactorily explain the reasons behind God's rules or His exceptions. People who do this sometimes get burned.

When using an electric griddle, I tell my preschoolers rather emphatically: "DO NOT TOUCH THIS! IT WILL BURN YOU!"

Astute kids who notice that Mom touches it herself (to pull it from the cabinet) might conclude that they know the real rule: "It's only hot if it's plugged in." Right? OUCH!

As it turns out, the griddle can still be hot long after Mom unplugs it. Their attempt to rationalize around the rule is dangerous because it stems from an incomplete understanding of the situation. My simple rule was calculated to perfectly protect the kids in all situations.

The children might observe another contradiction between my rule and my behavior. To test the warming griddle, I have sometimes lightly tapped the hot griddle with my fingertip, but I don't get burned. They might not notice that before I tapped the griddle, I licked my finger so the thin water barrier would absorb the heat. I don't elaborate on thermal dynamics because I don't want my kids experimenting with this procedure. My simple rule will fully protect them. But a child might conclude that the REAL rule is, "It's okay to tap the griddle if you haven't started the pancakes yet." OUCH again!

My kids are encouraged to ask me any questions they want, and over time I'll teach them the technicalities. But they often think they're ready before they really are. If they try to instruct each other by substituting their own reasons for my rules, they'll very likely oversimplify with dangerous results.

Jehovah tells the Israelites not to kill but later says to destroy Jericho. Huh? Plural marriages were usually condemned, except when allowed.[57] Huh? Do we avoid coffee due to tannic acid, or caffeine? Uh, I really don't know.

I'd better be careful about trying to supply the "why" behind God's commandments. I'll probably oversimplify. I may do harm if I don't separate my opinion from revealed fact. And if somebody offers me a questionable explanation for why God is doing such-and-such, I don't feel obliged to believe it.

I'll be the barbarian Grandma.

Studying prophets and Saints in early Church history always makes me wonder about how future historians might piece together my own life and motivations.

What will they think of the angry letter that I wrote (but never sent)? How will they process the rants in my journal (about circumstances that resolved just hours later in ways I forgot to record)? How many hasty opinions—that I vocalized forcefully but promptly regretted—live on in the memories or journals of my acquaintances?

Might I have accidentally and incorrectly maligned someone else in scattered writing or idle comments? I know a man who suddenly resigned a managerial position under suspicious circumstances, refusing to discuss the particulars. In private conversation I later discovered he had done this nobly and unselfishly to protect innocent parties. I've wondered how many employee e-mails speculate about his misdeeds.

So much behavior is enmeshed with cultural context. Think of today's sweet elementary school teacher who brings to the Halloween party a salad of "brains and eyeballs" (macaroni and skinned grapes). Everyone loves it. Yet wouldn't that likely seem gruesome to a future historian outside our culture? *She imitated the mutilation of dismembered bodies.*

My great-grandchildren may (hopefully!) live in the coming millennial world without contention or violence even between lions and lambs, in which no one learns war anymore. Will they be repulsed to find out that I sometimes ate bacon, chicken, and beef all in the same day? That I let my children play with swords and toy soldiers? I imagine them asking, "Grandma, how *could* you?"

After encountering some troubling perspectives about the Prophet Joseph Smith, I came across two books in which hundreds of his contemporaries recounted glowing stories of his daily kindnesses and courtesies. With conviction, these men and women testified that he was upright, honorable, commendable, and charitable.[58] After reading them, I too wanted to shout "Praise to the man!"

Will my own life be so full of kind and noble deeds that hundreds would defend me from skeptical historians?

Seeming contradictions
can resolve simply.

I find it helpful to remember that today's seeming inconsistencies may someday be explained very simply, as in the following examples.

King Zedekiah dismissed prophetic warnings, likely rationalizing that they were contradictory anyway. Jeremiah had warned that Nebuchadnezzar would lead Zedekiah to Babylon.[59] Ezekiel told Zedekiah that he would not see Babylon.[60] So which one should Zedekiah trust? In the end, the Lord fulfilled the words of both prophets: "And they slew the sons of Zedekiah before his eyes, and put out the eyes of Zedekiah, and bound him with fetters of brass, and carried him to Babylon."[61]

Matthew 2 tells us that the Jews had conflicting prophecies about where Jesus would come from.[62] The prophets had stated He would be called a Nazarene, that He would be born in Bethlehem, and that He would come out of Egypt. In hindsight, we know that all three of these prophecies occurred. Yet those confused by the apparent contradiction included even the Apostle Nathaniel. He expected Jesus to come from elsewhere, for he asked, "Can there any good thing come out of Nazareth?"[63]

Scientific debates about creation, age of the earth, and other related things always remind me of an analogy by Nobel physicist Richard Feynman.[64] He said discovering scientific law is like watching the gods play chess and trying to guess the rules. We observe that each piece moves by established pattern. For example, the rook always travels in a straight line. When our guesses about the rules seem to hold firm across many situations, they are often assumed to be facts. But wait! How can a rook jump over a king? (Castling!) And how can that pawn suddenly become a queen? (On the last square of the opposing side.) The basic rules we observed are still true, but there are simply times when other rules create exceptions.

Henry Eyring, famous chemist and father of President Henry B. Eyring, once said, "There are all kinds of contradictions in religion that I don't understand, but I find the same kinds of contradictions in science, and I haven't decided to apostatize from science."[65]

Solid evidence
sometimes isn't.

Answers Will Come 65

Ancient non-believers cited solid historical evidence to prove Christ's Resurrection must be a hoax. The elders of the Jews "gave large money unto the soldiers, Saying, Say ye, His disciples came by night, and stole him away while we slept. . . . So they took the money, and did as they were taught; and this saying is commonly reported among the Jews until this day."[66]

Could such blatant dishonesty create false evidence today? Here's an abridged excerpt from my mom's personal history:

> In 1985 there was a great deal of speculation and interest about a newly discovered letter written by Martin Harris to W. W. Phelps. It described Joseph Smith being led to the gold plates by a salamander, rather than by the angel Moroni. Forgery and handwriting experts declared its authenticity, and the Church had considered purchasing it from rare document dealer Mark Hoffman. Sadly, I heard of people leaving the Church over this.
>
> That same fall, I was deeply disturbed by the murders of two well-respected LDS members in separate pipe bombings. While I was working in the Church Office Building, a manager ran out of his office, announcing that a car had just exploded in the street below. I recall looking down at the billowing smoke, tears in my eyes, thinking, "When will it end?"
>
> Soon the truth came out: Mark Hoffman, the third "victim," was the killer of the first two. The bomb he'd been preparing for his next victim had detonated accidentally in his own car. Police found bomb-making materials in his trunk and later, forgery and counterfeiting materials at his home. The "Salamander letter" was a fraud. I never understood the convoluted motives for Hoffman's murders, but his forgery was apparently motivated by financial greed and a desire to embarrass the Church.
>
> Years later, I discovered Hoffman had forged other documents I had wondered about, including a falsified transcription of Joseph Smith promising the presidency of the Church to his son. I had wondered about that account many times over the years without knowing it was false to begin with.
>
> I wonder how many other forged documents are likewise still circulating around, confusing and deceiving people.[67]

CHAPTER 5

Pondering Prophets' Perspectives

"Prophets need tutoring, as do we all. However, this is something the Lord seems quite able to manage without requiring a host of helpers. The Lord provides discreet but needed feedback, as He did to Peter by the shattering sound of a rooster crowing."

—Neal A. Maxwell[68]

I hope they are allowed
occasional mistakes.

Imagine carrying ALL these apostolic burdens *for decades*:

First, advanced age along with the ordinary burdens of life.

The usual stuff. Your (and your wife's) surgical and medical procedures multiply into dozens of doctor appointments. Your washing machine breaks. You have car problems. Your sister needs help. There is no escape from paperwork.

Second, the burdens of being a public figure.

The Internet will forever retain, scrutinize, and criticize Every. Single. Word. You. Utter. You are never left alone in public. Exhausting formality surrounds you. It is difficult to joke or chat with natural candor. No matter how many hands you shake, you neglect hundreds of people. You can't remember everyone's names. Or every detail from unending presentations made by helpful Church employees.

Third, the burdens of administering a worldwide church.

Every single natural disaster, terrorist activity, economic crisis, and political instability affects people within your stewardship, often people you know personally. Your decisions must consider every nation's changing laws, currency fluctuations, market forces, visa requirements, and so on. You must reach unanimity on complex international problems with fourteen other strong-minded men of different backgrounds. You have jet lag from endless travel. (As just one example, President Boyd K. Packer visited fourteen nations one September and didn't sleep normally until Christmas.[69])

Fourth, the burdens of spiritual responsibility for millions.

You know tragic details behind sealing cancellations. In hundreds of interviews and blessings and mission calls, you must discern by the Spirit what God desires. You must speak endlessly on doctrines you've taught before. (Moses was so weary of people not listening that he wanted to die.[70])

Fifth, the burdens of seership.

God may show you weighty things you cannot share. Nephi and Daniel both grieved[71] because of destructions they had seen in vision, and Isaiah called it a burden.[72]

It's hard to imagine the real weight of the apostolic calling.

Seers still live
among us.

I used to wonder if Apostles still have revelations like Joseph Smith used to. Here are just a few reasons why I no longer wonder:

President Boyd K. Packer said, "The one most precious and sacred truth that I have to offer is my special witness of Jesus Christ. He lives. *I know He lives. I am His witness.* And of Him I can testify. He is our Savior, our Redeemer. Of this I am certain. Of this I bear witness in the name of Jesus Christ, amen."[73]

He also stated, "Joseph Smith and Sidney Rigdon recorded the following . . . 'this is the testimony, last of all, which we give of him: That he lives! For we saw him' (D&C 76:22–23).

"Their words are my words. . . . I bear my witness that the Savior lives. I know the Lord. I am His witness. . . . I bear my special witness in all humility but with absolute certainty, in the name of Jesus Christ, amen."[74]

President Henry B. Eyring said, "*I am a witness of the Resurrection of the Lord as surely as if I had been there in the evening with the two disciples in the house on Emmaus road. I know that He lives as surely as did Joseph Smith* when he saw the Father and the Son in the light of a brilliant morning in a grove of trees in Palmyra."[75]

Elder David A. Bednar stated, "I witness and testify that He lives. I know He knows us by name and is concerned about us in our individual circumstances. *I witness that He is resurrected.* It is the joy of my life to know that I will spend my life declaring that witness all over the world."[76]

And when asked the biggest challenge facing the Church and what should be done about it, Elder Ronald A. Rasband said, "One of the great blessings about having prophets, seers and revelators is that word *seer. And they're able to look into the future*; they're able to speak at times like general conference; and for two sessions now, we've been hearing a response to your question."[77]

Seers are often
forbidden to tell.

Repeatedly, the Lord has forbidden His prophets to tell certain things they know. Alma says many who know God's mysteries "are laid under a strict command that they shall not impart" except as specifically granted by God.[78] Mormon was forbidden to share many things,[79] including most of Christ's teachings to the Nephites. He explained, "Behold, I was about to write them, all which were engraven upon the plates of Nephi, but the Lord forbade it, saying: I will try the faith of my people."[80]

After Nephi saw the tree of life and Christ's ministry, he was shown the last days but forbidden to write about them: "And also others who have been, to them hath he shown all things, and they have written them; and they are sealed up to come forth . . . in the own due time of the Lord. . . . And behold, I Nephi, am forbidden that I should write the remainder of the things which I saw and heard . . . and I have written but a small part of the things which I saw."[81]

Apparently, Nephi could have written more about the final scenes before the Second Coming. The brother of Jared, Mosiah, and Moroni could have too but were commanded not to.[82] Christ told Moroni that He would only reveal to us the all-encompassing visions of the brother of Jared in "the day that they shall repent . . . that they shall exercise faith in me."[83]

I don't know what the Brethren today might be forbidden to share. If they seem collectively quiet on certain subjects, they may have received instructions similar to those given Nephi. When pressed for details on revelations he had received, President Boyd K. Packer often echoed the simple answer he had learned from Elder Marion G. Romney: *I do not tell all I know. If I did, the Lord could not trust me.*[84]

"For tonight, kids,
the babysitter's rules
are the law."

When I have my daughter babysit the other children, they sometimes ask, "How come *she* gets to be in charge?" I tell them it's because I trust she will be obedient to my requests, and has the sense and experience to keep them safe. I know she may not govern perfectly on a given night, but I still expect them to obey her as they would me.

She's still learning, but she has proven capable of handling needed situations, and when in doubt, she can call my cell phone for clarification. I tell the kids that their reward (or punishment) will depend on the report she gives me of their behavior. I allow her some freedom to govern within my rules:

They can watch any video in this drawer. Put the little ones to bed between 6:00 and 8:00, whenever they seem sleepy. A snack is okay if you want. Don't forget prayers and teeth brushing.

God never leaves us, of course. But I still think He authorizes prophets the way I do my babysitter. Within the rules, they have some freedom to govern as they see fit. Meanwhile, the Lord expects even mountains and angels to obey the prophet's direction. He told Nephi (son of Helaman): "I declare unto thee in the presence of mine angels that ye shall have power over this people . . . And if ye shall say unto this mountain, Be thou cast down . . . it shall be done."[85]

And He told Joseph Smith: "Whatsoever you seal on earth shall be sealed in heaven . . . whomsoever you bless I will bless, and whomsoever you curse I will curse."[86]

Some folks challenge Church policies or procedures by saying they are "just the prophet's own ideas," assuming this makes them somehow less binding than God's officially declared revelation. But a prophet with sealing keys can issue any instructions he deems necessary, even to the mountains. He can change the policy too, if circumstances warrant, but until he does so, it remains fully binding upon Church members.

If I trust God's judgment, then I can assume He has structured that privilege carefully so as to stay within His own rules, and that He's very careful about who receives this authority.

It's possible to miss
miracles in plain view.

I skip boring articles. For example, I would skim right past this routine report from the September 1997 *Ensign*: "In an auditorium designed to seat 800, more than 1,100 people gathered for the 18 May 1997 dedication of the new Brazil Missionary Training Center in São Paulo. Elder Russell M. Nelson of the Quorum of the Twelve Apostles gave remarks in English and then offered the dedicatory prayer in Portuguese. Also in attendance were Elder Harold G. Hillam of the Presidency of the Seventy and Elder Dallas N. Archibald."[87]

I was in Brazil when this event occurred, though I was not at the meeting. A new member named Gloria told me about her experience at the dedication. She said that Elder Nelson had relied on a translator during the first half of the meeting but then dismissed him. She wept while reverently recounting how Elder Nelson read the dedicatory prayer: "Sister! He spoke *perfect* Portuguese!"

President Russell M. Nelson is a gifted linguist who prepares carefully for foreign visits, but he is not fluent in Portuguese.

In June 1997, the *Church News* reported this event very modestly, under a very boring headline: "New Brazil MTC capable of housing 750 missionaries."

> After addressing the more than 1,000 people who attended the dedication of the Brazil Missionary Training Center in Sao Paulo, Elder Russell M. Nelson of the Quorum of Twelve offered the dedicatory prayer in Portuguese.
>
> "I feel the faith of those present, and my faith is strong enough that I will be able to deliver the dedicatory prayer in your native language," he told the congregation attending the ceremony.[88]

This reminds me of another understatement from Elder Dallin H. Oaks in the April 2010 general conference: "Miracles happen when the authority of the priesthood is used to bless the sick. I have experienced these miracles. As a boy and as a man I have seen healings as miraculous as any recorded in the scriptures, and so have many of you."[89]

I wonder: How many publically reported miracles did I not catch because I skimmed too quickly and too casually?

I question better
as WE, the Church,
not THEY, the Church.

"Why did *they* do that?"
Distances me from Church leaders.
Implies I don't belong to the group;
that I would do differently.

"Why did *we* do that?"
We are on the same team.
Though I don't know the particulars,
we must have our reasons for the decision.

Even when we love and sustain the Apostles themselves, we sometimes find it easy to be less supportive of local leaders or of the Church employees who necessarily manage various products and processes. But I'm learning there's a better way.

In January 2003 I repeatedly grumbled about the new fonts, white space, and margins in the *Ensign*: *Why did they change this layout? Don't they know it takes more time to read now? What were they thinking?!*

In March 2003, the *Ensign's* editors explained their reasons.[90] International readers had been waiting several months longer than English-speaking readers to get the same articles and general conference reports. This occurred because translations differ in length, so new visual elements and graphic layouts had to be designed for each language.

Now, sophisticated technology could adapt font requirements for many languages within the same page layout. Adopting extra white space in some languages allowed for more complicated or dense translations in other languages to fit within the same graphic layout. Saints could now receive their magazines in fifty-one different languages simultaneously.

Oops! *They* were, in fact, inspired to make the change. *They* had better reasons than I did. And after all, would it really hurt me that much to slow down my study? I quickly wished that instead of speaking as though something was wrong with "those editors over there," I had demonstrated enough faith to say: *"Hmm. I wonder why we've changed the layout."*

Then, when the reasons became apparent, I could feel unity, delight, and pride that *my* Church organization was so attuned to multicultural circumstances that *we* would be internationally inclusive, even in *our* choice of layout.

Joining the Church makes me part of "the body of Christ" in which "there should be no schism."[91] Talking about the rest of the body as *they* instead of *we* could ultimately be as harmful and sad as a handful of cells dissenting from the rest of the body. Ouch—that means I was acting like a cancer.

CHAPTER 6

Visualizing Eternity through Metaphors

"And that same sociality which exists among us here will exist among us there, only it will be coupled with eternal glory, which glory we do not now enjoy."

—D&C 130:2

Embryos don't eat salsa,
tell jokes,
build snow forts,
play the guitar,
light fireworks,
polka,
or hit home runs.

Because my mother died when I was ten, I relied heavily and gratefully on the doctrine that in the holy temple, families can be sealed together for all eternity. It was indescribably comforting to know that, through our temple covenants, she was still my mom and always would be. Jesus said that without these sealing ties, "the whole earth would be utterly wasted at his coming."[92]

Yet when I worried about whether God could be trusted, I began to feel serious anxieties even about the nature of heaven. We don't know much about how eternal families function. At that point in my life I wasn't sure I'd like having children on earth, let alone in eternity. Would I even like heaven? Would it be worth the effort? What exactly does a celestial woman do?[93] I've since heard similar concerns from many sisters, including some dealing with same-sex attraction.

Modern prophets teach that we are gods in embryo,[94] so let's first think about that comparison for a moment. Embryos (or at least fetuses) already share much of the physical anatomy of their parents and soon begin to have some of the same capabilities, such as movement, hearing, and even very limited sight.

But while embryos carry the raw DNA potential to become adults, they hardly have an adult-like existence. They don't drive, ski, invent, paint, congregate, quilt, procreate, play basketball, hike, bicycle, or compose music. Thousands of joys specific to adult life are simply unknown to the babe in a womb, or even to a toddler. If you described to a fetus the process of birth, it might sound hellish. No more umbilical cord or warm amniotic fluid? Mother far away? No thank you. I'll just stay right here as long as possible.

In the same way, the vast majority of celestial joys and capabilities must be simply beyond our wildest imaginations at this embryonic stage of our existence.

Seeds in a packet
can't fathom
forest life.

I have a mother waiting in the spirit world and a stepmother who has blessed me here on earth. I relate to people who feel concern about how eternal families play out—especially given complicated sealing situations involving multiple spouses, blended families, divorce, remarriage, and step-relationships. It has helped me to envision gods-in-embryo another way.

A Church-produced seminary video[95] illustrates how man can be "nothing" compared to God, and still have potential to be like Him. It shows a tiny seed, only a few millimeters in length, that is essentially "nothing" compared to the tree it can one day become: a giant sequoia, *seventy stories tall*.

Watching the video, I realized that family members are like many seeds "sealed" together in small packets. We are crowded by some seeds, separated from others, and sometimes uncomfortable with the jostling. In the dark, we might envision *together forever* from our squashed arrangements, tightly confined by time and space.

Imagine our surprise when the Lord pulls all of us from our many packets into the blinding light of heaven and "plants" us according to our sealing configurations. Our forest includes the whole Church of the First-born—sealed together from Adam down—embarking together on the wonders of eternity.

Encircled by those we're sealed to—those we already know and love—we experience a complete transformation. The Lord drenches us with living water and surrounds us with nourishing "earth." Our souls expand into thousands of layers of vascular matter and fiber. Reaching toward individual godhood, we climb far higher than giant sequoias. As through photosynthesis, we create sweetness from light itself. We reproduce painlessly and beautifully—throwing off pinecones by the thousands. In our overlapping branches, we enjoy antics of birds, squirrels, and other wildlife through endless gratifying seasons.

Redwood trees hold each other strong against the wind because the roots of the whole grove intertwine.[96] That's how I imagine eternal families: swaying together in a magnificent support network of intertwined roots and branches that ultimately reach in infinite directions.

More than 5,772 miles
beckon beyond the keyhole.

Increasingly, I'm helped by comparing eternity with the Trans-Siberian Railway—the world's longest. This eight-day journey covers 5,772 miles and six time zones from Moscow to Vladivostok, then on to China, Mongolia, and North Korea.

Imagine that we mortals sit paused somewhere in the middle, behind a door at a wayside train station, peering through the keyhole for a glimpse. We might see only drab passenger cars, patches of snow and wire fences.

From our keyhole, we could see nothing of the vast Lake Baikal, the largest inland lake, with her ferries and surrounding mountain tunnels. We would see nothing of the grand architecture at Irkutsk and Yekaterinburg, or the incredible bridge over the Kama River, near Perm. We'd have no view of the forested Ural Mountains, as well as literally hundreds of towns, pastures, and farmlands still out of sight.

Mortals' best data and logic at the keyhole cannot begin to comprehend our majestic journey known fully only to God. We grasp only a few short seasons—childhood, adolescence, child-bearing-years, old age—any of which can be marred or forfeited through heart-wrenching circumstances.

God summons us to look beyond these brief stages, with their snow and fences, and believe in the grandeur of the other 5,772 miles. His servants declare the hopeful message[97] that the scope of our eternal identities vastly exceeds what we see here, and that our families play a central part in the "Creator's plan for the eternal destiny of His children."

How many other significant seasons have eternal men and eternal women already passed through before mortal inputs arrived? How many other stunning and unique vistas lie ahead that we once joyfully anticipated but can't now remember? I believe it would be a mistake to give up on the journey based on the view at the keyhole. Apostles urge us to "stay in the boat" (the Good Ship Zion).[98] Perhaps they would also say, "Don't abandon the train" on God's narrow track toward the magnificent scenery awaiting.

"Eye hath not seen nor ear heard neither have entered into the heart of man, the things which God hath prepared for them that love him."[99]

Some things I'm saving
for when I can do them BIG.

Even if I had unlimited money and no family demands, I would still lament with the song that I've "only got a hundred years to live."[100] Mine is a persistent problem—yearning.

I want to explore Asia like Susan, blog like Emily, learn physics like Matt, volunteer like Judi, sew like Laura, sing like Aubrey, and garden like Mom. I want to earn a doctorate like Laurel, start a nonprofit like Mary, compose a musical like Janice, and make godly movies like Alex Kendrick. I need 10,000 hours to work on each talent. And that's just the beginning. I want to develop all the friendships I've begun. I want to read all the books on my list.

No matter what I choose, worthwhile talents, friends, projects, and destinations slip past me.

My daughter is exactly like me. Her high school offers more than sixty different courses, all valuable. She schemes about which seven to sign up for this year. Exasperated, we bemoan that the two best classes are scheduled during the same time block. It isn't fair. We strategize, feebly, the best we can.

Which classes will be cheaper now versus later? Which will be more enjoyable in college? Which friends and teachers go with which class? What prerequisites do we have to consider? What will be challenging enough? What fun classes will balance overload?

Life may last long enough to dabble a little in each area but not to master them all. Eternity may sound trite or too far away to some, but to me it has become my indispensable lifeline, an almost daily comfort. By God's grace, every opportunity still awaits me, just around the corner, with infinite time for enjoying it.[101] This doesn't always save me from being impatient for these experiences, but it keeps me from mourning their loss altogether.

Did Heavenly Father likewise help me strategize about my individual coursework for this life, as I do for my daughter?

You don't have to do this in the same order as your siblings. You don't have to do it all this semester. Given these prerequisites and required subjects, you've got a challenging load already. Save some electives for the next life when you can do them bigger with more resources. Let's consider which friends and teachers go with which classes. I'm excited for your growth this year.

Maybe I've already
been a CEO.
I can't remember.

It is my personal opinion that the veil has been drawn for each of us individually in a way that allows us to use some of our eternal talents more than others. I have passionately loved singing and performance since age three. Yet I was born with only a modest voice and limited ear. I believe this talent is already part of my eternal soul but is not meant to be the focus of my earthly mission. So for now, it's limited.

The longing I feel for growth in other areas now outside my reach might in some cases be *saudade*, the Portuguese word for fond, wistful remembering—a nostalgic homesickness for the happiness of a former moment. Some of the opportunities I can't have now may, in fact, be those that I enjoyed for eons before this life.

Am I just taking a recess from galactic music, fractal neurology, and black hole design? I can't recall. To what extent did Heavenly Father let me play in His creation laboratories? I don't know. Every exalted woman and man will one day be more capable and savvy than earth's prime ministers. Did I already have an internship to start learning those skills, now withheld behind the veil? Or is that season still ahead?

We are taught that before birth we "received [our] first lessons in the world of spirits, and were prepared to come forth in the due time of the Lord."[102] Those lessons apparently prepared us for our spiritual and temporal missions. But perhaps we also studied talents not for immediate use here but for use hereafter.

I like to think that in the matriarch coursework of heaven, God's daughters once studied numerous methods of nurturing, even more varied and diverse than is manifest in females within the animal kingdom on earth. A few such nurturing styles may apply in the seasons of my life here and now. Others may apply in greater measure later.

Meanwhile, it's nice to consider that some of the things I yearn for may already be inside me, tucked away for reuse in some delightful surprise tomorrow.

Master musicians
blend melodies
from different octaves.

As we continue on the path toward exaltation, today's gender stereo-types and limitations will necessarily evaporate. No celestial man will be helpless in the kitchen and no celestial woman will lose her sense of direction. Men must learn perfect nurturing and women must learn mechanical wizardry.

"They who dwell in his presence are the Church of the Firstborn. . . . And he makes them equal in power, and in might, and in dominion."[103]

Christ will share His inherited omniscience and omnipotence with all the joint-heirs.[104] So gender distinctions are not really about capabilities or limitations but about something else. If we're all made perfect, then what can be the differences between us? And to what purpose?

The three beings in the Godhead share the attributes of perfection but play very different roles. It's as though they are all masterful musicians, but they sing different songs. Or more approximately, they play different instruments that sound wonderful together in the same song.

I imagine godly men and women do the same.

For example, matriarchs were foreordained to provide the ordinance of physical birth and perform related duties.[105] Patriarchs were foreordained to provide the ordinances of spiritual birth and perform related duties. Both men and women harness God's power in performing these roles.

To me, this sounds as though men and women are singing the same notes but at different moments, in different octaves. Matriarchs sing treble. Patriarchs sing bass. Their similar melodies complement and echo each other, interweaving in gorgeous harmonies, like the sophisticated counter-point compositions of the preeminent composer J.S. Bach.

When our limitations are removed and we're perfected, our separate melodies might touch upon all the same themes, with all the same rhythms and melodies. But we might play them in different orders that complement and harmonize with each other. Just for fun. Just for beauty. Just for the joy of it.

Scratches disappear
during remastering.

Eternity together doesn't sound as exciting when sealing links include people whose current imperfections we find challenging. In such moments, I've found peace in this analogy shared with me by a dear friend:

> My mom's a really good person, and she's temple worthy. But as she has aged, she keeps getting stuck on certain compulsive habits and fixations that cause the family frustration and exasperation instead of love. After once praying for help about this, I visited Mom and saw her generously reaching out to another family member. In that hour, pure love and compassion from heaven filled my heart. I felt again the adoration I'd felt for her in my childhood. I saw her through God's eyes: a person who had unselfishly and honorably handled hard things in mortality. I feared the loving euphoria would evaporate during the coming days for the usual reasons. So that night I prayed God would give me something to hold on to that would help me remember.
>
> An image came to mind: a compact disc that had been dragged along the ground, now covered with scratches. This caused playback to repeatedly get stuck on certain notes, making it impossible to enjoy the original songs.
>
> Like the CD, my mom had been dragged through thorny days of mortality. Her annoying scratches weren't really part of her true eternal song. They were just the result of living through earth life. I realized that my annoyance didn't stem from dislike at all. Rather, somewhere down deep I remembered Mom's beautiful song—what it was supposed to sound like—and found the discrepancy painful between that and today's situation.

I love this analogy. I'm surely likewise scratched by hang-ups and idiosyncrasies that invite irritation. In the resurrection, I believe Christ will essentially "digitally remaster" every willing, repentant person. He can recreate for us a brand-new, incorruptible version of our original, uniquely sparkling music, improved somehow by the mortal experiences we have gained. When I'm at last able to hear the perfected songs of all the people in my sealing chain, I suppose the resulting symphony will be like a familiar melody that has been masterfully orchestrated into a new and improved, unimaginably beautiful love.

CHAPTER 7

Finding Strength for Obedience

"And they shall also be crowned with blessings from above,
yea, and with commandments not a few."

—D&C 59:4

Sign me up
for flight school.

Say you've been using a skateboard[106] to get around town. No license required. No rules. No hassle. And, um, not much power.

The Lord comes and offers you a car, 100 percent free to you. He will also pay for instruction, drivers' licensing, taxes, insurance, and unlimited gas. Enjoy. Grace. On the house. All that's required of you is a willingness to pass the driver safety exam and obey traffic laws thereafter. Excited, you accept. Soon you're loving the freedom of driving coast-to-coast.

The Lord returns, offering next a jet airplane, absolutely free, complete with paid gas, maintenance, airport fees, and full tuition for flight school. You'll have to follow lots of rules, restrictions, and regulations; certification requires time; you must demonstrate strict obedience to air traffic control.[107] But it's all yours, if you want it. You can cross oceans, landing anywhere in the world at will. Want to?

We choose a skateboard when we refuse God's help, determined to get by on our own power rather than obey higher principles. We choose a car by accepting basic biblical commandments like honesty and kindness. Such obedience harnesses more power and helps us steer a useful course toward Christ. We can go a long way, but it's just the beginning. Metaphorically, there are oceans we still can't cross. We opt for the pilot's license when we accept the restored gospel, Church organization, and temple covenants. These grant heavenly power and freedom for eternity.

By Christ's gift to us, all of God's children are invited to own an airplane and complete flight school, free of charge. Grace. But still we must act; we must try to learn to fly. We must study and practice, and practice, and practice. We will not be allowed to fly until we demonstrate obedience to covenants.

I wonder: is the spirit world like NASA training? More commandments for more freedom and power? Rules for planet creation, anyone? I suppose that coming ordinances, such as resurrection, will be associated with further covenants. Do I love obedience enough yet?

"And ye shall know the truth, and the truth shall make you free."[108]

I give Him:
my all

He gives me:

HIS ALL

I was a middle-aged mom before I grasped that the oath and covenant of the priesthood was not a list of duties to be studied in elders quorum. That name refers to verses I had overlooked (see D&C 84:35–40) because as a woman I do not hold an *office*[109] in either the Aaronic or Melchizedek priesthoods.

Yet this recorded, sworn oath, from God the Father Himself, applies to women as well as men. In the temple, both men and women dress in the robes of the priesthood. Both men and women participate in the ordinances of the Aaronic and Melchizedek priesthoods. We prepare to be priests and priestesses eternally. Therefore, these powerful verses are God's binding promise to me and to all who accept temple covenants, as long as they receive the prophets:

> Whoso is faithful unto the obtaining of these two priesthoods of which I have spoken, and the magnifying their calling, are sanctified by the Spirit . . . [and become] the elect of God.
>
> And also all they who receive this priesthood receive me, saith the Lord; For he that receiveth my servants receiveth me; and he that receiveth me receiveth my Father; And he that receiveth my Father receiveth my Father's kingdom; *therefore all that my Father hath shall be given unto him*. And this is according to the oath and covenant which belongeth to the priesthood. Therefore, all those who receive the priesthood, receive this *oath and covenant of my Father, which he cannot break*, neither can it be moved.[110]

God's generosity astounds me. As I consecrate everything I have to Him, He likewise consecrates everything He has to me. I bring to the altar all my pathetic little efforts, my pitiful best attempts, my puny sacrifices. He brings His universes, His omniscience, His righteousness, all the heights and depths that He has already conquered. He offers them to me.

My temple recommend is like a gift card for a billion dollars. I never want to lose it or misplace it in my priorities. I want to help my children receive and cherish their own. I feel the privilege—and the priority—of helping extend these blessings to those on the other side of the veil, who likely understand their scope much better than I do.

If the house
I'm about to buy
emits radon gas,
please warn me!

Warning! High voltage! Electrical hazard! Strangulation hazard! Bio-hazard! Shock hazard! Choking hazard! Danger! Radiation!

Because we know each person's life is valuable, we're careful to alert everyone to invisible dangers. We don't post signs to be bossy, annoying, superior, or prideful. We do it out of love.

As we strive to protect people, correct labeling is essential. When people overdose on drugs, their survival requires a correct diagnosis. The best way to care for them, lovingly and compassionately, is first to call it what it is.

God is trying to care for us compassionately too, and protect us from unseen spiritual hazards. He labels them very clearly: Sin.

The word *sin* means: Danger! This path looks innocent, but it will spiritually poison and eventually deaden you. Because I love you, I'm warning you. Don't touch this!

Or, in scriptural words: "If my people shall sow filthiness they shall reap the chaff thereof in the whirlwind; and the effect thereof is poison."[111] "Then when lust hath conceived, it bringeth forth sin: and sin, when it is finished, bringeth forth death."[112]

Media outlets now refer to adultery as merely "an indiscretion." Incorrect labels hide the danger. (Just be more "discreet" next time.) Satan has taught the world that it's judgmental to call anything a sin. Therefore, when we teach about sin, we should always clarify:

1. The word *sin* doesn't mean sinners are inherently evil, unlovable, or damned. It means their actions will hurt them. Everyone is worthwhile, and therefore everyone is worth warning.

2. The main concern isn't consequences for society in general but rather the sad consequences that will come to the person sinning, and his or her family and friends.

3. Some poisons (like radiation or lead) act invisibly or very slowly, but the end result is still sure.

Some obedience blessings
are things that
never happened.

I rarely talk to myself out loud. But on March 16, 2011, while shopping for my husband's birthday, I twice said aloud to myself, *"I should just go home."* But I didn't. Half an hour later I started home in my husband's car. After only a few streets I had to tell him by phone that I had crashed his car in traffic. Happy Birthday, Hubby.

You would think I'd recognize the next similar prompting, but no. A week later in a church meeting, I distinctly thought, *"I should walk out in the hall right now."* By ignoring that direction, I landed myself in a social fiasco too embarrassing and irrelevant to relate here.

But once I got it right. After a careful search for uplifting reading, I curled up with a popular Christian novel by well-respected authors. Chapter One was gripping, enjoyable, and appropriate—nothing amiss by Church standards. So I was surprised to receive a prompting to discontinue reading. I tried to ignore the prompting, but after a few pages (of nothing objectionable) the Spirit pressed so strongly that I relented and returned the book, unfinished, to the library.

A few years later, a sister in Relief Society shared an experience similar to mine. She recounted how the Spirit told her to put down a book, even though it seemed clean and appropriate by gospel standards. She obeyed, as I had.

After class, I curiously asked her the name of the book. It was the same title I had likewise started and returned. We both marveled at this second witness of the Spirit's instruction. Did the Lord spare us a persistent or crippling doubt? A recurring nightmare? We still don't know.

Though the Lord must allow some catastrophes, He certainly protects me more often than I acknowledge. Do I give thanks often enough for invisible blessings? Thanks for the angel that keeps my washing machine running. Thanks for steering the angry gunman away from our elementary school. Thanks for the germs we didn't catch. Thanks for the wars (or family rifts) that never started because someone's heart softened. Thanks for the gasoline shortage that didn't materialize. Thanks for the tsunami that didn't hit. For the persecution I didn't experience. For the outlet that didn't catch fire.

You don't tell an angel, "I'm too busy."

It's fairy-tale material. One dark night, I begin to settle in comfortably for the evening. Perhaps I am halfway through a meal. Perhaps I have plans for the evening that I don't wish to disturb or rearrange. There is a knock at the door, and when I open it, there stands someone who looks very ordinary and commonplace. She asks if she can come in and sit by my fire for an hour or so. She doesn't seem to have anything very special to offer and it is so inconvenient tonight that I am about to turn her away.

Then suddenly, I remember the old stories about magical gifts bestowed upon people who host traveling strangers. I wonder, "Will some special curse or blessing fall upon me based on my decision here tonight?"

She certainly doesn't look like a fairy godmother or enchantress. Of course, there is another possibility. I faintly remember a biblical passage: "Be not forgetful to entertain strangers: for thereby some have entertained angels unawares."[113]

Could this average-looking woman, so human in her manner, possibly be sent as a ministering angel to me and my family? Do I let her in for the hour? Do I wait to see what she offers, or what unique blessings later befall me? Or do I turn her away, impatient with her slow manner or personal idiosyncrasies? Do I consider myself already too busy or too strong to need her?

She says she is my visiting teacher.

> *"Verily, verily, I say unto you, as I said unto my disciples, where two or three are gathered together in my name, as touching one thing, behold, there will I be in the midst of them—even so am I in the midst of you."[114]*

I'll do it for Jesus.

As I read the New Testament one weary day, these verses suddenly become very personal to me. It is as though I am standing at the foot of the cross just before Jesus dies. He speaks to Mary and then to John: "When Jesus therefore saw his mother, and the disciple standing by, whom he loved, he saith unto his mother, Woman, behold thy son! Then saith he to the disciple, Behold thy mother! And from that hour that disciple took her unto his own home."[115]

In my mind's eye there is another woman standing some distance away. She looks as though she might be Jesus's sister or cousin or aunt. I visualize Jesus fixing His gaze on me. With absolute and penetrating clarity, He says to me, nodding back to her, "Behold thy sister!"

Perceiving the Lord's request, do I dare to really "behold" this unfamiliar woman? Do I behold her in the manner of one who truly wants to see her? Do I watch for who she is, and what she cares about, and what she feels and needs? Or do I merely glance casually at her and then look away?

Will I go to her, as John did, that same hour? Will I consider my responsibility to her as seriously as if she were my own blood sister? Will I wrap my arms around her? What if she tries to rebuff me? What if she acts disinterested or annoyed by my attentions? What if she lets me in but talks much too long?

Will I keep going back? Will I keep visiting for months and years just because Jesus asked me to watch over her? Will I try to nourish her in the gospel as I knew the Lord meant for me to do?

I hope so.

And when Jesus's next direction arrives on another slip of paper from the Relief Society president, will I do it, again, for Him?

I hope so.

I'm just on
the helping chair.

Sharing the gospel: A single conversation can never do it justice. The gospel is just too BIG. What if my missionary efforts start at the wrong end? I don't want to ruin someone's eternity because of my clumsiness.

Meanwhile, I find myself baking with my little daughter. I could work much faster without her, but she loves standing on the "helping chair" and stirring in ingredients one by one as I hand them to her. Now dump. Stir. Pour. Stir. Good girl!

When she spills awkwardly, I adjust by adding more. When she lets eggshells fall in, I fish them out. I take care of the ingredient ratios, temperatures, and cooking times for different recipes. Too young to understand the complexities of the process, my daughter just licks the spoon and asks when she can taste the cookies. The oven seems to take forever.

I begin to think about my missionary efforts. I guess I'm not the main chef in that labor. I'm on the helping chair. The Lord could do it all much faster Himself, but He enjoys teaching me. His Spirit prompts me to add a missionary invitation to conversations here and there. "Now stir gently," He whispers. "Add a testimony. Now stir again. Good girl!"

So often, I spill awkwardly, saying too much or too little. Have I ruined my friend's impression of the Church forever?

The Lord reassures me that He can compensate. He knows the ingredient ratios: what reading material my friend will see, her history and prayers, what her family members will say, and how to mix them for best results. I just need to keep following His promptings one by one.

I don't know which efforts produce quick results and which will take a long time. The Lord is the main cook, and He monitors the complex interactions of faith and agency. He knows when to stir people along and when to let them sit and rise awhile. To me, this process often seems to take forever.

Along the way, I'm learning little things about the process of saving souls, like what makes friendships sweet or sticky. I'm learning to trust that the Lord can fix my errors. I've already tasted some joy in His kitchen. I look forward to tasting the final results of our labors.[116]

"Showers of blessings" await sheep.

As I strive to be loyal to teachings from Church leaders and to turn away from other voices, some people will call me a sheep. They will say I'm in the Church due to crowd pressure and can't think for myself.

They're right about one thing: I desperately want to be a sheep. But they don't understand why: because I've heard the music of heaven. Elder Wilford W. Anderson explained, "There are those who ridicule members of the Church for the things we do. That is understandable. Those who dance often appear strange or awkward . . . to those who cannot hear the music."[117]

My heart has come to both hear and sing Psalms 23: "The Lord is my shepherd; I shall not want. He maketh me to lie down in green pastures: he leadeth me beside the still waters. He restoreth my soul . . . my cup runneth over . . ."[118]

I'm not very good yet at hearing my Shepherd. I wander too much. But I've tasted green pasture, and now I crave more. Whereas the voices of Internet rapids churn with brash contentions, the Brethren at general conference echo Jesus's own words in a manner epitomizing still water for the soul. They help me hear the music behind the Savior's promises to all willing to be called His sheep: "He shall feed his flock like a shepherd: he shall gather the lambs with his arm, and carry them in his bosom, and shall gently lead those that are with young."[119]

> For thus saith the Lord God; Behold, I, even I, will both search my sheep, and seek them out . . . and will deliver them out of all places where they have been scattered in the cloudy and dark day . . . I will feed them in a good pasture, and upon the high mountains of Israel shall their fold be . . . I will . . . bind up that which was broken, and will strengthen that which was sick . . . they shall no more be a prey. . . . And I will make with them a covenant of peace, and will cause the evil beasts to cease out of the land: and they shall dwell safely in the wilderness . . . and I will cause the shower to come down in his season; there shall be showers of blessing.[120]

"I am the good shepherd. . . . I lay down my life for the sheep."[121]

Covenants liberate us
from exclusions.

I love it that the Lord frequently refers to Himself as the bridegroom and the covenant people as the bride.[122]

"For thy maker, thy husband, the Lord of Hosts is his name . . . my kindness shall not depart from thee, neither shall the covenant of my peace be removed, saith the Lord."[123]

As I work on my relationship with the Lord, it helps to remember this marriage analogy. A bride might be disappointed when her new husband does not respond exactly the way she expects. But it is better to talk it out directly with him rather than complain to her friends. In like manner, I may find moments when it feels the Lord has let me down by not responding the way I wanted. But talking it out with Him is much more effective than complaining to my friends.

And when the bridegroom is as faithful and devoted as the Lord, it would be tragic for a bride to abandon her covenants when things seem hard. Satan tries to hide this truth by making covenants feel like a trap—like an insurance policy with hidden exclusions. He whispers to covenant-keeping members, "You didn't really know what you were getting into. You didn't understand all that was required."

Of course we didn't. No one *ever* knows what the future will hold. We don't know how we'll be affected by Church callings, employment changes, illnesses, death, disabilities, natural disasters, financial troubles, or political instability. The Lord rarely tells anyone in advance what will be required.

But the beauty of having a covenant is that it covers all contingencies. It is not a contract with spelled-out limitations. I won't suddenly hit the outer edges of grace. Christ's new and everlasting covenant sends grace flowing into every possible perilous moment in my future. His promise is even stronger than "for better or for worse, for richer, for poorer, in sickness and in health." He assures me that no height or depth or tribulation or distress or persecution or peril or death or things present or things to come will be able to separate me from His strength and guidance.[124]

He is willing to stand with me, no matter what, forever. My happiness, safety, and security depend on keeping my promise to stand with Him, no matter what, forever.

CHAPTER 8

Winning Brain Battles

"The battle today, between Babylon and Zion, is being waged
between the synapses of our brains."

—Tina Peterson[125]

I'm streaming content
from many sources.

My brain is basically a mobile device for my spirit.[126] As the administrator, my spirit decides which apps to run, what data is worth streaming, and what content to install or delete. There are many sources.

1. I create some content myself by putting daily experiences into my internal memory. Some of those include movies, songs, conversations, practiced talents, job training, scriptures, trivia.

2. Some notifications, messages, and downloads stream in through the Holy Ghost. I want more of these. They often interact with scriptures, hymns, and lessons I have already stored in internal memory. Heaven is respectful of my agency and usually waits for me to invite the download.

3. Some content streams in from Satan's temptation channels, assaulting me with pop-up invitations at inopportune moments. I have sometimes downloaded content containing Satan's adware and malware intrusively built into apps that look innocent. I'm trying to learn to detect and uninstall these.

4. Many brain inputs are essential system processes that run in the background. These include such things as blood sugar, nutrition, sleep, adrenaline, and other hormones. They often stall or need updates. When system processes are disabled or malfunctioning, fine-tuned spiritual streaming and other important applications are often temporarily immobilized until the problem is resolved. Sometimes, as with clinical depression or other mental illness, professional expertise or medication can be key to restoring functionality.

5. I also have irrelevant passing thoughts that resemble inconsequential options flashing by in an app store.

As my spirit learns to administer my brain-device, I continually have to practice identifying which sources are influencing my current thinking. Not every thought or feeling that passes through my heart or mind represents my own true self. As Shannon L. Alder puts it, *"Feelings are something you have; not something you are."*[127]

Hormones provide
great spiritual exercise.

GRRRR! Don't mess with me! I'm so mad I could fight a tiger. The problem is, there's no enemy in front of me. The baby wailed at 3:00 a.m. When I jumped out of bed to help him, I suddenly felt angry. Who am I angry at?

The baby is certainly innocent. The only other person nearby is my husband. I start to feel angry at him, for, uh, not helping more.

Except that's ridiculous. My Prince Charming is a wonderful helper, and I specifically urged him to sleep through night-time feedings this week so he could meet work deadlines.

So why am I angry? Did Satan pounce the moment I awoke? Is my spirit really this grumbly and uncharitable?

Not really. Adrenaline is the culprit here. The old fight-or-flight hormone floods into my bloodstream when I need instant strength—especially when I'm tired or running on low blood sugar. Though Satan hopes I'll run the wrong way with it, adrenaline's original purpose is to help me flee a fire. Or pull a crashed car off my child. Or jump up for 3:00 a.m. feedings.

I just get too strong a dose sometimes. Until the extra energy drains away, I'll churn inside like I'm in battle instead of in bed. My spirit has to practice charity and rational thinking until the surge passes. After about twenty minutes, it does.

The Lord did something amazing for the Three Nephites: "There was a change wrought upon them, insomuch that Satan could have no power over them . . . that they were holy, and that the powers of the earth could not hold them."[128]

If the Lord wanted to, He could instantly put me beyond the tug of adrenaline, estrogen, and every other hormone or chemical that plays on my brain and body. Since He's chosen not to, there must be a reason for this struggling.

Olympians sometimes swim in sweats to increase the drag and work their muscles harder. This mortal body may often be like that too. Some of the challenges that I process as temptations are more helpfully viewed as mortal processes that provide for my spirit an intensive training exercise in patience, self-discipline, and charity.

I'm on a light diet.
Nothing rotting.

Following my sense of smell is critical to physical survival. Yummy smells (cinnamon!) help me recognize tasty food. Nasty smells (diapers!) alert me to decay, sewage, and poison.

Should I keep or discard the leftovers lurking inside the fridge? I take a whiff. Hmmm. Questionable. Should I eat it, and chance food poisoning—or just throw it out? Past episodes of vomiting have taught me: No more rotting food.

When it comes to soul food, I want to eat, drink, and breathe light from heaven, because "that body was which is filled with light comprehendeth all things."[129] Before I consume a blog, video, or article about Church issues, I take a whiff. Does it smell strongly of cynicism, bitterness, or decaying faith? President Russell M. Nelson described this requirement for last days' spiritual survival: "As we diligently focus on the Savior and then follow His pattern of focusing on joy, we need to avoid those things that can interrupt our joy . . . anything that opposes Christ or His doctrine. . . . That includes the philosophies of men, so abundant online and in the blogosphere, which do exactly what Korihor did."[130]

My belief in Christ and His kingdom provides real joy. Korihor-style philosophies[131] interrupt that by sneering at testimony, denying divine guidance for the Church, and assuming that Church leaders' actions are motivated primarily by self-interest or dishonesty. I want none of this.

God will sometimes prompt me to respond to critical perspectives, hard stories, and sensitive issues when He sees that light can enter there. But without light, I might spend endless research hours pursuing angles that don't bless or edify me. Or worse, angles that tragically distract me from higher purposes while I try to detoxify from spiritual decay.

If a blog or video digs up the Brethren's weaknesses like gossip, disdains the legitimacy of personal spiritual witnesses, or seeks to sow seeds of suspicion and distrust, it can hardly be a loyal advisor to me. No good. Toss it.

"The people of Ammon . . . were more wise than many of the Nephites;
for they took [Korihor] and bound him and . . . caused that
he should be carried out of the land.[132]

When in battle smoke,
don't give the Book of Mormon
equal time.
Give it twice the time.

I can't avoid every mist of darkness, but I try hard to avoid breathing them voluntarily. When my Internet browsing leads me to something of questionable intent, I've learned not to consume the whole thing just for curiosity or idle interest.

On several occasions, people I love have found Internet contentions choking their faith. They have called and asked me to process it with them. During the first few times this happened, I struggled to determine how I could best embrace loved ones without letting the contention affect my heart too. Cub Scout Fire Safety Day answered my prayers.

> "Without a full oxygen tank, you won't survive the smoke," firefighter John told the Scouts.
>
> "You have to carry twice the oxygen you would normally use. This oxygen tank could sustain me for thirty minutes at resting heart rate. But it will only last for fifteen minutes in a fire, because my body is working hard under stress. I go in with a buddy and a time limit. If my oxygen runs low or I become immobilized, alarms go off so that my buddy can pull me back to safety. Then someone else takes the next rescue shift.
>
> "We only go into a fire as a last resort. And we only go in after we've put on all of our special protective clothing."

Those firefighters' regulations have become mine too. Before I agree to read or watch anything suggested by a doubting loved one, I fill my tank with twice as much time in the Book of Mormon and general conference *Ensign*. Then the Holy Ghost goes into the conversation with me. Sometimes, He has instructed me to pull back and not continue any further into the smoke. Sometimes He has let me quickly see how to help someone exit safely into spiritual fresh air.

I also feel protection when I dress in white temple clothing and renew my covenants in the Lord's house. Temple ordinances help me identify the smokescreen philosophies of men. Temptations to grumble about Church leaders evaporate. Mists of darkness blow away.

"Whoso would hearken unto the word of God, and would hold fast unto it, they would never perish; neither could the temptations and fiery darts of the adversary overpower them."[133]

The toddler can say 5 words:
"da" (dad)
"daw" (dog)
"ma" (mom)
"fla" (flag)
"ba" (ball)

But the toddler understands 216 words: cup, chair, head, hair, neck, cheek, nose, toes, fingers, thumb, hands, feet, tummy, ears, eyes, elbow, arm, shoes, shirt, pants, socks, bath, let-the-water-out, water, down, up, want, peas, peanut-butter-balls, book, couch, kitchen, bedroom, bathroom, outside, stairs, car, truck, rabbit, dog, cat, bird, dance, music, TV, milk, juice, cracker, graham cracker, cheese, ham, refrigerator, table, piano, popper, star, heart, circle, square, triangle, one, two, three, Jesus, temple, cloud, moon, sun, sky, ceiling, clock, toy, bear, butterfly, bicycle, pot, racket, rock, flower, tree, swing, slide, basketball, sit, basket, put, away, come, here, over there, library, diaper, diaper wipes, baptize, pray, prayer time, fold, kneel, close, open, door, mirror, towel, dry, wash, earrings, apple, street, sidewalk, fall, bump, okay, love, hug, kiss, baby, hat, glasses, sunglasses, listen, Cheerios, cereal, bowl, spoon, fork, thirsty, hungry, dirty, stinky, clean, pretty, comb, brush, teeth, tongue, toothbrush, toothpaste, fan, telephone, phone, computer, light, window, train, blanket, bed, crib, balloon, dolly, give, take, let, watch, stay, walk, stroller, sleep, loud, hot, cold, touch, point, paper, toilet paper, wipe, keys, come, go, happy, clap, pat, grass, carpet, pillow, scriptures, stop, no, stop sign, sign, red, yellow, hurt, boots, box, cabinet, cans, then, grandma, grandpa, angel, turn, off, on, knees, legs, big, little, high, hello, good-bye, bye-bye, thank-you, very, good, children, around, splash, yes, spider, fly, airplane, soap, church, song, stand up, lions.

When it comes to the language of the Spirit, we're pretty much like toddlers. We often understand spiritual things in ways that surpass our ability to describe them to others. Elder Neal A. Maxwell said, "We have been taught more than we can tell, for the language used is not that which tongue can transmit."[134]

I have experienced this failure of words when I try to explain to my children how wonderful my grandparents were. I describe things that Grandma *said* or *did*, but I struggle to convey who she *was*. How her voice pulsed with intangibles. How her tone, her posture, her eyes proclaimed, "I love you and I value you!" How safe I felt there.

This is likely how prophets feel as they try to tell us about a visit from Jesus. They can describe a little of how He looks, but they cannot begin to convey the warmth, power, and majesty of His actual presence. Many of us who have not yet seen Jesus have also felt His presence or His direction in ways that don't translate well into English. We clearly feel what He's trying to tell us, but our verbal descriptions of those moments are stiff, hollow versions of the real thing.

Elder Boyd K. Packer described the dilemma this way: "We do not have the words (even the scriptures do not have words) which perfectly describe the Spirit. The scriptures generally use the word voice, which does not exactly fit. These delicate, refined spiritual communications are not seen with our eyes, nor heard with our ears. And even though it is described as a voice, it is a voice that one feels, more than one hears."[135]

From my own experiences, here's how I have falteringly tried to describe the experience of hearing the Lord's voice: feeling a message conveyed silently with perfect stillness, without any physical sensation, but somehow spiritually accompanied by an in-flowing grace and peace and clarity.

I wish there were a word for that.

I translate
spiritual feelings
into my words.

I *love* what Joseph Smith said of personal revelation: "All things whatsoever God . . . has seen fit and proper to reveal to us, while we are dwelling in mortality . . . *are revealed to our spirits precisely as though we had no bodies at all;* and those revelations which will save our spirits will save our bodies."[136]

God is sending messages to me exactly the same way He did before I was born. I don't need to *learn* the process. I just need to block out bodily and worldly distractions enough to remember the process. President Benson said, "Nothing is going to startle us more when we pass through the veil to the other side than to realize how well we know our Father and how familiar his face is to us."[137]

I expect that applies to His voice as well.

Apparently, God bypasses my physical brain, eyes, and ears—and talks straight to the core of my spirit. Sometimes He dictates specific words to me, but more often His messages arrive in something purer than earthly language. It's that *impression* or *prompting* we describe when we say we *just knew* that we should visit someone or stop doing something.

Now in mortality, when I want to describe a spiritual impression to someone, I have to put words on the feeling that came to me through spiritual channels. I essentially "translate" it from my first, native language (spirit) into my second language (English.)

But so much is lost in translation. At a loss for words, I might grasp for a trite phrase like, "from the bottom of my soul." Such wording can be misinterpreted as spiritually shallow. Yet the shallowness lies in the translation, not the original.

That's why it doesn't come out right if I try to tell others about my spiritual experiences without having the Holy Ghost there to help translate. That's also why I can't share some personal, sacred experiences with those making doubting or cynical comments on the Internet. Unless they allow the Holy Ghost to translate my typed words back into the native language of the Spirit, they will not understand. For this reason, I believe that the Internet vastly over-represents the numbers of the faithless and underrepresents the testimonies of the faithful.

I don't have to own
the mists of darkness.

We often use the word *temptation* in reference to chemical addictions or sexual attractions. In these contexts, Satan urges our physical appetites toward sin.

We speak less often of the temptation to doubt, the temptation to murmur, and the temptation to grumble. Occasionally, I have succumbed to these. What mechanics did Satan use to get the best of me in these temptations?

It is my personal opinion that Satan imitates the spirit-to-spirit channel from heaven with an insidious spirit-to-spirit channel of his own. I believe that sometimes his temptations don't arrive in specific words but rather as miniature mists of darkness hurled at my spirit like little black clouds.[138]

At time he tricks me because as I experience those dark impressions I unintentionally process them by translating them into my own words. Because the words come from me, the sentiment sounds like my own idea:

"I seriously doubt that."

"Church leaders don't really get what I'm going through."

"This church meeting feels like a waste of time."

When Satan gets me to doubt, murmur, or grumble in my own voice—with my own words—I don't as readily recognize the need to resist the ideas. I develop a warped view of my identity in relation to spiritual things.

I want to learn to catch that black temptation cloud and hurl it right back where it came from. I don't want to buy into the deception about who I really am and what I really believe.

Jesus said: "Pray always that you may come off conqueror; yea, that you may conquer Satan."[139] God says I can win this brain battle if I take all my doubts straight to Him. Prayer doesn't always remove the dark mist immediately, but it helps me remember its source.

Coming before God in prayer invites me to speak more reverently and carefully from the real me. My husband's mission president taught us, "Your real self is your best self."[140] The real me came from heaven as a disciple of Jesus Christ, determined to obey and finish well.

Accusing is the hallmark
of the devil.
The Lamb has already defeated him.

As I have worked to delete dark propaganda from my thinking, I've been deeply impressed by these verses from Revelation about the premortal war in heaven: "I heard a loud voice saying in heaven, Now is come salvation, and strength, and the kingdom of our God, and the power of his Christ: for *the accuser of our brethren is cast down, which accused them before our God day and night.* And they overcame him by the blood of the Lamb, and by the word of their testimony."[141]

I picture a bitterly jealous devil, evicted for constantly launching accusations, "day and night," at the leadership of heaven. I suppose he gained followers by chipping away at their trust in Heavenly Father and Jesus Christ, denouncing God's motives and purposes. I also suppose he accused us all of being too weak or foolish to make it back to heaven.

It seems to me that his tactics haven't changed. Satan is still flinging accusations at the Brethren. And he still jeers accusations at Latter-day Saints. He tells us that we're hypocritical and that we're narrow-minded. He especially hints maliciously to us, in those little black clouds of his, that we're not dedicated enough, loving enough, or good enough to belong in heaven.

We fight this battle over and over during this life, and sometimes discouragement or even depression overtakes us because of the weight of it all. But John saw the Saints overcome Satan by the blood of the Lamb. Our answer[142] to Satan's broadcasted accusations forever remains:

> True, we're not good enough yet. But Christ is. Through our covenant with Him, He will gather us under His wings. He will hold our right hand, strengthen us, and help us. His grace is sufficient to make weak things become strong unto us. He will wipe away all the tears from our eyes. He will restore, a hundredfold, all of our losses. He will go before and prepare the way for us. He will lead us along. He will enlighten our minds and fill our souls with joy. He will show us the mysteries and peaceable things. He will fight our battles. Indeed, through the Atonement, He has already fought our battles and won them all. In all these things, we are more than conquerors through Him who loved us.

Weighing Glory

"I do not know why we have the many trials that we have,
but it is my personal feeling that the reward is so great, so eternal
and everlasting, so joyful and beyond our understanding that
in that day of reward, we may feel to say to our merciful,
loving Father, "Was that all that was required?"

—Linda S. Reeves[143]

God leans on the scale.

An intellectual debate about the Church might circle like this:

Nonbeliever: *You can't prove Book of Mormon geography.*

Believer: *Not yet. But there's still strong evidence in chiasmus, Quetzalcoatl, and eleven witnesses.*

Nonbeliever: *And Egyptologists dispute Pearl of Great Price translations.*

Believer: *But Hugh Nibley details dozens of Pearl of Great Price parallels to recently discovered antiquities. . . .*

Observers who weigh both sides' evidence within their own hearts might watch the scales tip back and forth, back and forth, between belief and disbelief. Which side of the balance proves heaviest, of course, depends on how much weight each item receives, which is rightfully a personal decision.

I think in some cases God watches quietly while His children sort out their desires: *Do I want to believe? How much weight will I give to the faith side? How much effort? How much do I want His input on the questions, His fingers on the scale?*

Over the past few decades, I have been working through this slow process, trying to purify my desires through determined obedience. Periodically, on His own peculiar schedule, the Lord has added a gift of private, personalized evidence to the belief side of my heart. I still have internal struggles with faith, but now they settle out more like this:

My doubting self: *Why can't we figure out Book of Mormon geography?*

My believing self: *Remember the witness you received while reading at the kitchen table that incredible morning in 2007?*

My doubting self: *Why don't we see clearer revelation?*

My believing self: *What about last year's priesthood blessing that was perfectly fulfilled? And that night with Sister Lortz in the temple when you received unmistakable direction?*

In my own heart, the faith side of the balance has over the years sunk heavier and heavier into the stable realm called "knowing." Unanswered questions still exist, but their consequence on the doubt side is simply negligible compared to the cumulative and gracious weight of God's fingerprints.

The knowing keeps growing.

I *love* strawberries. I *love* my husband and children. Both declarations are true. Each one uses the word *love* appropriately, and it is the best word for the sentiment. Yet these sentences vastly differ in the amount and quality of love they represent. On an imaginary spectrum, strawberries sit far to the left, at "low-level love," and my husband and children sit far to the right, at "high-level love."

Even so, someone bereaved might warn me: "Just you wait. Someday you'll love your departed spouse and children stronger than you do now. The love spectrum is bigger than you think."

Then, from the spirit world, loved ones already reunited might whisper to the bereaved: "Just you wait. When you're together again here, you'll find the love spectrum is bigger and more beautiful than you think."

And then, resurrected beings might joyfully instruct those spirits, "Just you wait. You're just getting started on love. When you get to this stage, and your capacity increases, you'll find a love spectrum bigger than you can possibly imagine."

Elder Boyd K. Packer compared the declaration of love to the sharing of a testimony and explained: "When we are wont to put [our testimony] into words, we say it in the same way—all using the same words. The apostles declare it in the same phrases with the little Primary or Sunday School youngster. 'I know that God lives and I know that Jesus is the Christ.' We would do well not to disregard the testimonies of the prophets or of the children."[144]

Years ago, I could have truthfully told you that I knew the gospel was true. Today, I know it at a much higher point on the knowing spectrum. I'm not just convinced. I *know* it's true, at an exhilarating "high-level knowing"—akin to the deep soul love that I have for my husband and children. I'm aware that some know it better than I do. The spectrum is likely bigger than I think. Given the joyful certainty that has grown within me so far, I can't wait to find out what that means.

Savor invisible glory.

GLORY. It makes Bethlehem's shepherds sore afraid. Heavenly fire surrounds the burning bush, the wilderness tabernacle, and the Kirtland Temple. It astounds the captors of Nephi and Lehi. It consumes Elijah's sacrifice. It blinds Saul. It causes Joseph Smith to fear the grove will catch fire.

But there's another kind of glory. No fire. No blinding light. Nothing visible. Nephi says of Jesus's first coming: "[Jesus] went forth ministering unto the people, *in power and great glory*; and the multitudes were gathered together to hear him; and I beheld that they cast him out from among them."[145]

Christ simply put His hand on someone's eyes or head. He simply spoke words to a lame man, or a fig tree, or the wind. The healed people didn't suddenly glow like angels; they just returned from broken to normal. The "power and great glory" happened without fanfare in seemingly ordinary moments.

Saints in the last days know this kind of glory too: "I, Nephi, beheld the power of the Lamb of God, that it descended . . . upon the covenant people of the Lord . . . and they were armed with righteousness and *with the power of God in great glory*."[146]

I now see that I tasted invisible glory when visiting the Las Vegas Temple open house at age sixteen. On the way to the temple, we'd passed many casinos and bars. In contrast, the light, peace, and joy of the celestial room flooded over me so powerfully that I begged my parents to return the next day.

At age six, my son tasted it too. He met me at the car one day after church and said, "Mom, today I did the most important thing I've ever done at church!" Surprised, I asked him what that was. He replied, "I walked all around the halls and looked at every single picture of Jesus. I cried because I felt so happy. I'm crying a little bit now; can you see it?"

If we tried to make a movie about those life-changing moments, all you'd see is us smiling as we walked down a hallway. Powerful music might help. But it's impossible to fully depict the invisible glory that descends on people's hearts when God whispers to them. It is perfectly quiet, but Oh. So. Real.

Fan the sparks.

Having *an eye single to the glory of God*[147] doesn't just mean purifying our motives. It also means watching steadfastly for the glory of God around us, in all our ordinary living.

Glory is not a tangible or physical feeling for me. Some of my friends say they feel warmth in their chests during these experiences, but I almost never do. For me, it's like the spiritual air around me silently thickens with pure oxygen, increasing my capacity for joy. It's just a spiritual mix of love and light and happiness. It's real. It's nourishing.

I believe that all of God's children taste sparks of glory when they act in righteous, godly ways. It's that selfless joy when you cheer for a baby learning to walk or a young child learning to read. It's the satisfaction when you comfort the victim of a natural disaster, welcome a refugee, tend to the sick or elderly, or push someone in a wheelchair. It usually accompanies selfless ministering, as it did with Jesus.

As we make gospel covenants, the gift of the Holy Ghost seems to blow oxygen on these sparks, fanning them into a brightly burning joy that is *"unspeakable and full of glory."*[148]

I felt it when my husband and I were sealed for eternity. I felt it during the baby blessings and baptisms of my children. Glory surrounded our family during several months of unified indexing for FamilySearch. org. It shimmered invisibly when the missionaries taught my friend and her daughters. I felt it when I duplicated and shared my grandma's life history with my cousins. It has accompanied rare, special dreams that help me remember deceased loved ones, still nearby. It washes over me sometimes during endowment ordinances and sealing sessions in the holy temple. The feeling somehow whispers about the joy that will accompany heaven. It promises that the Lord is reserving something extraordinary.

As I reflect today on my life's path, I see how slowly piecing together the big picture has been a blessed process. Joy has accompanied the placement of each individual puzzle piece. God's glory hasn't yet illuminated all the details related to my questions. But He has let my spiritual eyes see, afar off, the joy and peace that will accompany them. And He has assured me that *answers will come.*

One parting thought . . .

Thank you for reading these pages.

Please let errors or weaknesses in this book strengthen your testimony of the Prophet Joseph Smith.

I have eighteen years of formal schooling. I have a laptop, word processing tools, an online thesaurus, and a digital gospel library. I received helpful suggestions from a dozen people. After every interruption or pause, I had to reread several paragraphs or pages to get back into the train of thought I had left. And after all of that, I still had to rework most pages many times to improve the flow and resolve inconsistencies in mood, tone, or logic. Writing this book took two years.

The Book of Mormon is twelve times longer and infinitely more complex and profound than this book. It involves hundreds of people, thousands of years of history, intricate Hebraic literary devices, powerful sermons, detailed foreshadowing, and complicated nuances of politics, economics, warfare, and human nature.

Joseph Smith had three years of formal schooling and no electronics. His wife said he dictated from no reference materials and never asked to have the prior sentences read back to him, even after long interruptions. He translated the Book of Mormon in about three months.[149]

I testify that he did that by the power of God.

Sources

*All scripture references and general conference addresses
are available at lds.org*

1 Fairmormon.org presents faithful answers to common claims made by anti-Mormon critics. Written and compiled by LDS scholars and apologists; it is not an official website of the Church. http://www.fairmormon.org/perspectives/publications/the-nature-of-prophets-and-prophecy-2.

2 This quote appears many places on the Internet, but I have been unable to find an original source. My apologies to Howard Johnson.

3 Numbers 16.

4 Numbers 20:7–13.

5 Jonah 3:1–2; 4:1–11.

6 Mark 10:13–14, Matthew 19:13–14, Luke 18:15–16.

7 Mark 9:33–34; Luke 9:46–47.

8 Luke 9:52–56.

9 John A. Tvedtnes catalogues many biblical parallels to modern anti-Mormon claims in his online article, "The Nature of Prophets and Prophecy," written for fairmormon.org. http://www.fairmormon.org/perspectives/publications/the-nature-of-prophets-and-prophecy-2.

10   Dinesh D'Souza, *What's So Great About Christianity?* (Washington, DC: Regnery, 2007), 206–214.

11   2 Kings 19:35.

12   Lynne Watkins Jorgensen and *BYU Studies* (1996) "The Mantle of the Prophet Joseph Passes to Brother Brigham: A Collective Spiritual Witness," *BYU Studies Quarterly*, 36:4 , Article 8. Available at: http://scholarsarchive.byu.edu/byusq/vol36/iss4/8

13   I highly recommend the online essay by J. Max Wilson, "Watchmen on the Tower—On the Limits of Prophetic Fallibility." Wilson makes a beautiful case for why modern prophets can be trusted despite their personal weaknesses and some historical errors. The essay is available at https://www.sixteensmallstones.org/watchmen-on-the-tower-on-the-limits-of-prophetic-fallibility/.

14   On this question, I especially appreciated C.S. Lewis's book, *The Problem of Pain* (New York: HarperCollins, 2001). Lewis acknowledges, "If I knew any way of escape [from pain] I would crawl through sewers to find it. . . . I am not arguing that pain is not painful. Pain hurts . . . I am only trying to show that the old Christian doctrine of being made 'perfect through suffering' is not incredible. To prove it palatable is beyond my design" (105).

15   I am forever indebted to black BYU professor Marcus Helvecio Tourinho de Assis Martins, who almost certainly would not even remember that several-hour interview with a struggling undergraduate. His powerful testimony of the Lord's love pointed all my painful doubts in the direction of hope. Among other testimonies he helped me to find were 224 recorded interviews with black members conducted by Jessie L. Embry in the book *Black Saints in a White Church: Contemporary African American Mormons* (Salt Lake City: Signature Books, 1994). See also *A Soul So Rebellious* by Mary Frances Sturlagson (Salt Lake City: Deseret Book Company, 1980).

16   Elder David A. Bednar, "Bear Up Their Burdens With Ease," *Ensign*, May 2014.

17   Eternal thanks to Jennifer Gillins Chapman and Elizabeth (Beth) Payne Harrison.

18 1 Nephi 4:17.

19 D&C 88:66.

20 2 Nephi 9:21.

21 Alma 7:11–12; Mosiah 14:3–5.

22 Alma 40:8; Moses 1:6.

23 Isaiah 49:16.

24 D&C 121:25.

25 Richard G. Scott, "The Transforming Power of Faith and Character," *Ensign,* Nov. 2010.

26 Job 38:7.

27 Joseph Smith, *Lectures on Faith*, Lecture First, vss. 15, 16.

28 Boyd K. Packer, "What Is Faith?" in *Faith* [1983], 42–43, as quoted in *Book of Mormon Student Manual Religion 121–122*, 224; emphasis added.

29 Neil L. Andersen, "Faith is Not by Chance, but by Choice," *Ensign*, Nov. 2015, 65, emphasis added.

30 1 Peter 1:7.

31 Ether 12:6.

32 Ether 4:4–10.

33 3 Nephi 26:11.

34 3 Nephi 12:1–2.

35 John 20:29.

36 D&C 10, 1 Nephi 19:1–3.

37 D&C 10:33, 43.

38 Alma 30:16.

39 Alma 8:31.

40 Quote from the movie *Faith Like Potatoes* (2006), distributed by Affirm Films; directed by Regardt van den Bergh.

41 D&C 98:1–3.

42　588 BC + 1828 AD = 2416 years. Nephi recorded the Lord's words in such detail as to include a phrase that Joseph himself forgot to report in our Pearl of Great Price. Compare JS—History 1:19 with 2 Nephi 27:25 and Isaiah 29.

43　1 Nephi 5:5.

44　Adam Kotter, "When Doubts and Questions Arise," *Ensign*, Mar 2015. Available at lds.org. The questions on this page are my own paraphrase of his ideas.

45　This quote is often attributed to Neal A. Maxwell, but I cannot find the source within the lds.org database. I think perhaps it originated as a book chapter by Richard Neitzel Holzapfel—"Questions, but No Doubts" in *Expressions of Faith: Testimonies of Latter-day Saint Scholars*, ed. Susan Easton Black, (Deseret Book Company, 1996).

46　Harold B. Lee, Conference Report, Apr. 1947, 50. Thanks to President David Glew of Wilmington, North Carolina, for bringing this principle to my attention.

47　1 Kings 17.

48　Moses 5:5–6.

49　Matthew 4:18–22.

50　D&C 95:8.

51　1 Nephi 2:7.

52　Leviticus 7:12; 2 Chronicles 29:31.

53　"Reverently and Meekly Now," *Hymns*, no. 185.

54　Jeremiah 29:11.

55　1 Nephi 17:7.

56　Isaiah 55:9.

57　Jacob 2:24–32.

58　Hyrum L. Andrus and Helen Mae Andrus, *They Knew The Prophet: Personal Accounts from Over 100 People Who Knew Joseph Smith* (Covenant Communications, 1974). Available through Amazon.com in Kindle format. Some out-of-print, used copies may also be available.

Also see Mark L. McConkie, *Remembering Joseph: Personal Recollections of Those Who Knew the Prophet Joseph Smith* (Salt Lake City: Deseret Book Company, 2003).

59   Jeremiah 32:4–5.

60   Ezekiel 12:13.

61   2 Kings 25:7.

62   Matthew 2:5, 15, 23.

63   John 1:46.

64   Richard Feynman, *The Pleasure of Finding Things Out: The Best Short Works of Richard Feynman* (Cambridge, Massachusetts: Perseus Books, 1999), 13–15. The whole analogy is delightful and goes far beyond the portion I summarized here.

65   Henry Eyring, *Reflections of a Scientist* (Salt Lake City: Deseret Book Company, 1983.

66   Matthew 28:12–15.

67   Memoir of Patricia Anne Wille Anderson; in the author's possession.

68   Neal A. Maxwell, "A Brother Offended," *Ensign*, May 1983.

69   Lucille Tate, *Boyd K. Packer: A Watchman on the Tower* (Salt Lake City: Bookcraft, Inc., 1995), 182.

70   Numbers 11:15.

71   1 Nephi 15:4–5; Daniel 7:15, 28.

72   Isaiah 13:1.

73   Boyd K. Packer, "These Things I Know," *Ensign*, May 2013; emphasis added.

74   Boyd K. Packer, "The Witness," General Conference address, April 2014. Emphasis added.

75   Henry B. Eyring, "Come unto Me," *Ensign*, May 2013; emphasis added.

76   David A. Bednar, Facebook post, Feb 2, 2016, at 12:26 p.m.; emphasis added.

77   Oct. 2015 press conference announcing three new apostles. Transcript available at: http://www.deseretnews.com/article/865638241/Complete-transcript-of-press-conference-with-3-new-LDS-apostles.html?pg=all.

78   Alma 12:9.

79   Mormon withheld names of the Three Nephites (3 Nephi 28:25). Moroni withheld details of evil oaths and combinations (Ether 8:20).

80   3 Nephi 26:11.

81   1 Nephi 14:26, 28.

82   Ether 4:1–7.

83   Ether 4:6, 7.

84   Tate, 178.

85   Helaman 10:6, 8, 9.

87   "New Missionary Training Center Dedicated in Brazil," News of the Church, *Ensign*, Sept. 1997.

88   "New Brazil MTC capable of housing 750 missionaries," *Church News*, June 14, 1997. http://www.ldschurchnewsarchive.com/articles/28786/New-Brazil-MTC-capable-of-housing-750-missionaries.html.

89   Dallin H. Oaks, "Healing the Sick," *Ensign*, May 2010.

90   "Our New Look," News of the Church, *Ensign*, March 2003.

91   1 Corinthians 12:25, 27.

92   D&C 2:3.

93   See the essay entitled "Mother in Heaven" at lds.org under the subheading "Gospel Topics." https://www.lds.org/topics/mother-in-heaven?lang=eng.

94   This chapter assumes that the Latter–day Saint reader is already familiar with doctrines surrounding eternal families and each person's divine potential. For more information on these topics, please visit lds.org under the subheading, "Gospel Topics," particularly the

essay entitled "Becoming Like God," https://www.lds.org/topics/becoming-like-god?lang=eng&_r=1#38.

95   "God's Work and Glory" referring to Moses 1:39, and described thus: "A tree-seed analogy helps show our divine potential." Produced by the Church Educational System.

96   Marilyn Batemen, "Being One With Christ," BYU devotional address, January 5, 1999.

97   "The Family: A Proclamation to the World," *Ensign*, Nov. 2010, 129.

98   Elder Russell M. Nelson, "Endure and Be Lifted Up," *Ensign*, May 1997: "As children of our Heavenly Father we may foolishly want to get 'out of the boat' before we arrive at destinations He would like us to reach." Elder Jeffrey R. Holland, "Abide in Me," *Ensign*, May 2004: "Stay in the boat, through squalls and stills, through storms and sunburn, because that is the only way to the promised land. This Church is the Lord's vehicle. . . ." Elder Russell M. Ballard, "God is at the Helm," *Ensign*, Nov. 2015, and "Stay in the Boat and Hold On!" *Ensign*, Nov. 2014: "[God] is at the helm, and His great and powerful ship flows toward salvation and exaltation. Remember that we cannot get there by jumping out of the boat and trying to swim there by ourselves. . . . Brothers and sisters, stay in the boat, use your life jackets, and hold on with both hands."

99   1 Corinthians 2:9.

100   Five For Fighting, "100 Years," from the album *100 Years*, Oct. 26, 2004.

101   Joseph Smith, Jr. "The King Follett Sermon." This version taken from *Documentary History of the Church*, 6:302–317, as follows: "You must begin with the first, and go on until you learn all the principles of exaltation. But it will be a great while after you have passed through the veil before you will have learned them. It is not all to be comprehended in this world; it will be a great work to learn our salvation and exaltation even beyond the grave."

102   D&C 138:56.

103   D&C 76:94–95.

104   Romans 8:17 and D&C 84:38.

105   In the family-based order of heaven, might "matriarch" be considered a form of priesthood office?

106   Thanks to my wonderful father, EksAyn Anderson, for teaching me this analogy.

107   See Dieter F. Uchtdorf, "Fourth Floor, Last Door," *Ensign*, Nov. 2016.

108   John 8:32.

109   As before, in the family-based order of heaven, might "matriarch" be considered a form of priesthood office?

110   D&C 84:35–40.

111   Mosiah 7:30.

112   James 1:15.

113   Hebrews 13:2.

114   D&C 6:32.

115   John 19:26–27.

116   Jacob 5:71.

117   Wilford W. Andersen, "The Music of the Gospel," *Ensign*, May 2015.

118   Psalms 23:1–4.

119   Isaiah 40:10–11.

120   Ezekiel 34: 11, 12, 14, 16, 22, 25, 26.

121   John 10:11,15.

122   Revelation 21:2, 9; Isaiah 62:5; D&C 33:17, 65:3, 88:92. The Lord sometimes laments when the bride deserts him: Lamentations 1:2; Ezekiel 23:5–9; Hosea 2:7.

123   3 Nephi 22:5, 10; Isaiah 54:4.

124   Romans 8:35–39.

125   Quoted in a blog post by Catherine A. (Last name not given),

"The Battle in Our Brains," January 26, 2012, at http://segullah. org/daily-special/the-battle-in-our-brains/. Catherine indicates the quote was given at a meeting of "The Mormon Women Project" during the year prior.

126 Another version of this analogy was given by Boyd K. Packer, who often said our brain is a stage and we decide what actors are allowed on it. "Inspiring Music—Worthy Thoughts," *Ensign*, Nov. 1973.

127 Shannon L. Alder, quotes for Goodreads. http://www.goodreads. com/quotes/906515-feelings-are-something-you-have-not-something-you-are.

128 3 Nephi 28:39.

129 D&C 88:67.

130 Russell M. Nelson, "Joy and Spiritual Survival," *Ensign*, Nov. 2016.

131 Alma 30:12-48.

132 Alma 30:19–21.

133 1 Nephi 15:24.

134 Neal A. Maxwell, "Patience," *Ensign*, Oct. 1980, 31.

135 Boyd K. Packer, "Candle of the Lord," *Ensign*, Jan. 1983.

136 Joseph Smith, Jr. "The King Follett Sermon." This version taken from *Documentary History of the Church*, 6:302–317.

137 Ezra Taft Benson, "Jesus Christ—Gifts and Expectations," *Speeches of the Year, 1974*, (Provo, UT: Brigham Young University Press, 1975), 313.

138 My ideas on this page and the next echo words from Joseph Fielding Smith: "Satan has power to place thoughts in our minds and to whisper to us in unspoken impressions; he plays upon our weaknesses." *Answers to Gospel Questions*, comp. Joseph Fielding Smith, Jr. (Salt Lake City: Deseret Book Company, 1957–1966), 3:81.

139 D&C 10:5.

140 Thanks to former mission president John Galbraith (Russia Novosibirsk Mission) for this profound quote.

141 Revelation 12: 10–11; emphasis added.

142 3 Nephi 10:6; Isaiah 41:13; Isaiah 41:10; Ether 12:27; Revelation 21:4; Matthew 19:29; D&C 49:27; John 14:1-3; D&C 78:18; D&C 11:13; D&C 42:61; D&C105:14; D&C 50:41; Romans 8:37.

143 Linda S. Reeves, "Worthy of Our Promised Blessings," *Ensign*, Nov. 2015, 9.

144 Boyd K. Packer, "The Spirit Beareth Record," *Ensign*, May 1971.

145 1 Nephi 11:28.

146 1 Nephi 14:14; emphasis added.

147 D&C 4:5, 88:67.

148 D&C 11:13; Helaman 5:44–45.

149 Gospel Topics essay on Book of Mormon translation, available at lds.org. https://www.lds.org/topics/book-of-mormon-translation?lang=eng#29.

About the Author

Shalissa Lindsay cherishes taking moonlit strolls with her husband, Nathan, making up nonsense songs with her eight kids, and chatting with treasured friends from the nine states in which she has lived (Utah, California, Texas, Virginia, Indiana, Michigan, North Carolina, Missouri, and Montana). She served a mission in São Paulo, Brazil, and holds degrees in human development and organizational behavior from Brigham Young University. Shalissa worked in change consulting and instructional design before becoming a full-time mom and a part-time author.